VICTOR BORGE
PIANIST-HUMORIST

TINI & CONSUELO
DANCING

DICK LASALLE
AND HIS ORCHESTRA

RK MONTE AND HIS CONTINENTALS

Two shows nightly .... 9:30 and 12:15.
Cover after 9:30—$2. Saturdays—$2.50.
Closed Sundays. SOMETHING NEW—a
special Persian Room Luncheon at $2.50.

THE PLAZA
FIFTH AVENUE AT 59TH STREET

VARIETY

glamorous s
of the
Persian Room

HAL KANNER & Orchestra
alternating with
Mark Monte's Continentals
TWO SHOWS NIGHTLY 9:30 and afte
the theatre at 12:30. Cover after 9:30—
$1.50, Saturdays—$2. No shows Mondays
SPECIAL SHOW SUNDAY NIGHTS

THE PLAZA
Plaza Circle at 59th Street

INTRODUCING THE YOUNG FRENCH SINGING STAR

Jacques Pearls

Famous
International
Entertainer

THE *Persian Room*
PRESENTS

AIR CONDITIONED
Persian Roo

CHO and his orchestra

The Persian Room Presents

The Persian Room Presents

An Oral History of New York's Most Magical Night Spot

PATTY FARMER

BEAUFORT BOOKS

Copyright © 2024 by Patty Farmer

FIRST EDITION

All rights reserved.

No part of this book may be reproduced in any form or by any electronic or mechanical means, including information storage and retrieval systems, without permission in writing from the publisher, except by a reviewer who may quote brief passages in a review.

ISBN: 9780825310423

For inquiries about volume orders, please contact:
Beaufort Books
sales@beaufortbooks.com

Published in the United States by Beaufort Books.
www.beaufortbooks.com

Distributed by Midpoint Trade Books
a division of Independent Publisher Group
https://www.ipgbook.com

Interior Design by Ashley Prine
Cover and interior illustrations by Sujean Rim

Printed in the United States of America

PHOTO CREDITS

Pg. 10, 62, 163 (Hildegarde), 226, 246 Henry Krupka of D'Arlene Studios, Inc., © Christina Krupka
Pg. 18, 180, 163 (Dinah Shore, Ethel Merman), 204 © Bettman/Corbis
Pg. 23, Museum of the City of New York Manuscripts and Ephemera Collection
Pg. 25, 46, 51, 69, 78, 148, 190, 195, 163 (Eartha Kitt), 209, 212, 221 Photofest, Inc.
Pg. 76 Courtesy of Andy Williams
Pg. 111, 116, 132, 145 Don Hunstein © Sony Music Entertainment
Pg. 154, 156 Courtesy of Michele Lee
Pg. 168 Courtesy of Betty Johnson Gray
Pg. 174 Courtesy of Cathryn Kenzel
Pg. 199 Courtesy of Carol Lawrence
Pg. 235 Courtesy of Jack Jones

To my friend Mitzi Gaynor

Although she never performed in *the Persian Room*, she has regaled me with endless Plaza stories—from staying there on her honeymoon with Jack Bean to insisting the studios put her up there while filming, to visiting with Mrs. Roosevelt, bumping into Marlon Brandon, and a countless array of other fun escapades.

Thank you, darling Mitzi, for adding even more color to my lifelong love affair with the storied Plaza Hotel.

CONTENTS

Introduction 9

CHAPTER ONE
The 1930s 17

CHAPTER TWO
The 1940s 29

CHAPTER THREE
The 1950s 61

CHAPTER FOUR
Jazz at the Plaza 103

CHAPTER FIVE
The Plaza on Record 119

CHAPTER SIX
The 1960s 137

CHAPTER SEVEN
The 1970s 203

Epilogue 245
Index 250
Acknowledgements 256

INTRODUCTION

The entrance to the Persian Room after its lavish 1950 transformation.

In 1955, after a successful career in entertainment, the legendary Kay Thompson dreamed up and introduced to the world a precocious six-year-old girl named Eloise, who lived at the elegant Plaza Hotel in New York City with her nanny and a few rather eccentric pets. With no parents in sight, Eloise concocted her own adventures and, throughout the course of six books, won the hearts of millions of children and adults worldwide, introducing them to the delights of the magical Plaza Hotel in the process. (Her picture—painted by the book series' illustrator Hilary Knight—still hangs prominently in the lobby, and to this day, many make a pilgrimage just to see the place this fictional force of nature turned upside down on a daily basis!)

Growing up, I was among those little girls who read about Eloise and dreamed of life at the Plaza—and guess what? Sometimes dreams *do* come true! Nowadays I am lucky enough to live in a condominium at the Plaza with my own singular menagerie: two fastidious and bossy teacup-size French poodles named Sabrina and Marina.

I may not have managed to score Eloise's penthouse, but I live in a lovely spot on the eighth floor overlooking Central Park. Snuggled on my window seat I can see the gaily hued canopy of the carousel in the summer and the bundled-up, red-faced skaters frolicking at Wollman Rink in the winter. Year round I hear the clop, clop, clop of the horse-drawn carriages that have been ferrying people around the neighborhood since the turn of the nineteenth century. Within a few short city blocks are some of the most fashionable stores; think Bergdorf Goodman and the original Saks Fifth Avenue, as well as many famous and world-class restaurants.

I love roaming around the building, most of which is still a bustling hotel and favorite New York City attraction. There's nothing better than taking tea under the breathtaking stained-glass dome over the Palm Court, unveiled for the first time since the 1950's, when Conrad Hilton had the ceiling dropped to accommodate newfangled air conditioning—the height of modern luxury at that time. Or enjoying a cocktail and bite in the elegant Oak Bar and Oak Room. (As I write this, these iconic meeting spots are shuttered—but I hear plans are in the works to reopen them soon, in grand fashion.) I never tire of being welcomed by our lovely doormen, in their fancy red coats festooned

FRED STERRY
President

JOHN D. OWEN
Manager

DISTINGUISHED by its world-famous reputation; ideally located on Fifth Avenue, facing the attractive vista of Central Park.

OFFERING its guests the unique privilege of quiet atmosphere with accessibility to fashionable shops and theatres.

•

Fifty-ninth Street and Fifth Avenue.

The PLAZA *New York*

Life at the Plaza is the best—but there's one beautiful part of it that exists only in memory: the Persian Room.

with gold braid. And here's the best part: like Eloise, I can summon room service whenever I want—though I tend to order more than the six raisins she favored.

Today, if you visit the Champagne Bar and Rose Room, you are standing where the Persian Room used to be—and what a unique and marvelous place it was! For some reason, Kay Thompson never allowed Eloise to sneak into the Persian Room—although she herself performed there many times and it is precisely where Eloise was conceived. (But I am getting ahead of myself; you'll learn all about that from Hilary Knight later in the book.) I can easily imagine the spunky six-year-old spying on its elegant patrons and performers from underneath its tablecloths or behind its fancy draperies.

For more than forty years, from 1934 to 1975, the Persian Room was the place to be. An unparalleled array of performers graced its stage—anyone who was anyone in entertainment was thrilled to accept an engagement. And, though almost five decades have passed since the final ovation, there are many who remember this extravagant nightclub. Because I dearly love my home and its history, I want to take you on a magical, delightful journey back to those halcyon days of refinement and sophistication. Come along as we step into a time when ladies and gentlemen were chic and debonair, when everyone was coiffed and made up and ready for the time of their lives. At the Persian Room, the couple at the next table might be Elizabeth Taylor and Richard Burton, Frank Sinatra and Ava Gardner, Katharine Hepburn and Spencer Tracy, or John F. Kennedy and Jackie.

Or perhaps you'd spot the celebrated chanteuse Hildegarde on a night away from performing there herself.

I can't wait to introduce you to the people who knew firsthand what it was like to entertain and be entertained in the Persian Room. I talked to as many of them as I could find, and they were extremely happy to share their stories.

What are we waiting for? Let's begin our journey at the beginning.

CHAPTER ONE

The 1930s

Lillian Gaertner Palmedo puts the finishing touches on one of her murals, specially commissioned by designer Joseph Urban, in anticipation of the Persian Room's 1934 opening.

In 1934, the country was emerging from the Depression. Prohibition had finally been repealed, and Henry Rost, the operating manager of the Plaza, seized the opportunity to shake things up at the landmark hotel and bid adieu to the no-alcohol policy. He decided to create a stylish room where fashionable people could meet for cocktails, dinner, and dancing. He believed that if he could get the details just right, it would become a "hot spot"—a destination for celebrities and socialites as well as the cherished guests of the hotel.

To realize his vision, Rost knew he needed more than a conventional architect or interior designer. He hired Ziegfeld Follies scene designer Joseph Urban to transform the former Rose Room into something truly special: a kind of nightly sojourn to exotic Persia. With characteristic flair, Urban adorned the walls with five exquisite murals by Lillian Palmedo,

The dance team of Sally and Tony De Marco. Tony and another wife, Renée, were the first performers at the Persian Room, on April 1, 1934.

depicting luxuriant scenes of hunting, dancing, singing, eating, and drinking, Persian-style. Red dominated the color scheme, from the crimson velvet drapes and plush ruby-colored chairs to the burgundy-dappled carpets, and all was splashed with vivid blue accents. As his crowning touch, Urban installed a massive twenty-seven-foot bar to celebrate the demise of Prohibition. Many of the artists I spoke with commented that the bandstand was unusual in that it was set at ground level—flush with the diminutive round tables. Like some other night spots, entertainers made their entrances through the kitchen. Carol Channing confessed to me that she was always a tad tardy hitting the stage because the tantalizing smells enticed her to stop for a quick nibble before greeting the crowd.

On April 1, 1934, the Persian Room officially opened with an afternoon benefit for the New York Infirmary for Women and Children. That evening the Renee and Tony De Marco dance team, accompanied by the Emil Coleman Orchestra, entertained the swank crowd into the early hours of the morning. In the audience was an assortment of personalities: socialites, captains of industry, royalty, and New York debutantes with their beaus. Small linen-draped tables were set with china, crystal, and gleaming monogrammed silver flatware. Huge bouquets scented the room, and the chandeliers, festooned with thousands of dangling teardrop crystals, sent sparkles everywhere. The price of this night on the town? Three dollars for dinner and the show, or $1.50 for supper only. But really, who would want to eat and

THE COLORFUL NEW PERSIAN ROOM IN THE HOTEL PLAZA

AT *New York's* SMARTEST SUPPER CLUBS
THEY ARE SAYING SEAGRAM'S

As final curtains fall in Broadway theaters, ermine-coated women and their silk-hatted escorts start for an after-theater rendezvous. As Park Avenue dinner parties end, knowing hosts suggest their favorite place to dance. Wherever this may be, wherever they may go ~ ~ as in their homes ~ ~ their choice is Seagram's. For among smart people today, you find a preference for Seagram's. Word has spread that the House of Seagram holds millions of gallons of fully matured Canadian and American whiskies, assuring an unvarying, continuous supply. If your taste is for American whiskey, you will praise Seagram's "Ancient Bottle" Rye and Seagram's Bourbon. Both, mellowed by five years of aging, were distilled in Canada by American experts and bottled in bond under Canadian Government supervision. They are full-bodied, full strength, 100 proof ~ ~ Should you prefer the distinctive flavor and subtle bouquet of Canadian whiskey, you will enjoy Seagram's famous "V. O." and Seagram's "83" ~ ~ All of these fine whiskies come to you from the House of Seagram — from the largest treasure of fully aged Rye and Bourbon whiskies in the world.

Bottled in Bond
UNDER CANADIAN GOVERNMENT SUPERVISION

YOU WILL ENJOY—
SEAGRAM'S CELEBRATED LONDON DRY GIN
SEAGRAM'S KING ARTHUR LONDON DRY GIN
AND SEAGRAM'S MODERATELY
PRICED BLENDED WHISKIES:
SEAGRAM'S 7 CROWN
SEAGRAM'S 5 CROWN

Say **Seagram's** *and be sure*
FINE WHISKIES SINCE 1857

This advertisement is not intended to offer this product for sale or delivery in any state or community wherein the advertising, sale or use thereof is unlawful.

A 1935 Seagram's ad featuring the most glamorous nightspot in the Big Apple.

DAISIES

Gin .... .55
   Gin, Grenadine, Lemon Juice, Fruit
Sloe Gin .... .65
   Sloe Gin, Grenadine, Lemon Juice, Fruit
Brandy .... .90
   Brandy, Grenadine, Lemon Juice, Fruit
Rum .... .65
   Jamaica Rum, Grenadine, Lemon Juice, Fruit

JULEPS

Mint .... .85
   Bourbon Whiskey, Sugar, Brandy Top, Fresh Mint
Brandy 1.10
   Brandy, Sugar, Rum Top, Fresh Mint
Major Bailey .... .85
   Gin, Sugar, Fresh Mint, Lemon Juice

LONG DRINKS

Amer Picon .... .70
   Amer Picon, Grenadine or Curaçao, Carbonic
Black Velvet 1.70
   Split of Guinness's Sto... Champagne
Gin Buck ....
   Gin, Lemon Juice, Split
Horse's Neck ....
   Imp. Ginger Ale, Wh...
Mamie Taylor ....
   Scotch, Lime and Lim... Peel, Ginger Ale
Pernod à l'Eau (Ab...
   Pernod, Lump of Su...
Rum Collins ....
   Rum, Lemon Juice,
Tom Collins ....
   Gin, Lemon Juice,
Brandy Collins ....
   Brandy, Lemon Ju...

Drink List

The Persian Room at the Plaza

A Persian Room drink menu from 1936..

run? Newspapers praised the opening as "the best night club soirée since Prohibition ended."

For the remainder of the 1930s and well into the '40s, exhibition dancing and big band orchestras were the main attractions at the Persian Room and other fashionable nightclubs.

The comic dance team of Paul and Grace Hartman tickled Persian Room audiences through the 1930s and 40s.

The De Marco dance team featured Tony along with a series of partners—his successive wives—throughout the 1930s and '40s. Nina was followed by Renee and then Sally. It was Renee who appeared with Tony at the Persian Room that historic opening night, and on several other occasions until 1940. Interestingly, all three teams were reviewed as among the most successful exhibition ballroom dancers.

Veloz and Yolanda were another pair of nationally acclaimed ballroom dancers that graced the Persian Room stage. Yolanda Casazza was born in New York's "Little Italy" in 1908. She met Frank Veloz at a roadside speakeasy in 1920, and though it wasn't an instant love match, they liked to dance together and soon had racked up more than forty trophies from dance contests. They married and were known

Eddy Duchin tickles the Persian Room ivoriesas John Roosevelt and Sally Clark join the fun.

for their fabulous costumes—designed by Frank—and their improvisational style. Their exhibitions at the Persian Room were great fun because they were virtually unrehearsed and different each time.

Between rounds of the club circuit, Veloz and Yolanda opened dance studios in Southern California and danced in such films as *Champagne Waltz* (1937), *Pride of the Yankees*

(1942), and *Cavalcade of Dance* (1943), for which they earned an Oscar nomination.

Leo Reisman led the most sought-after "society" orchestra of the period. Born in 1897, he began studying the violin at age ten, and by the time he was a young teenager, he was playing in hotel bands. At twenty-two, he established his own band and performed at many of New York's best venues, including the Persian Room. He recorded more than eighty hits, including *Stormy Weather* (1933) and *You Kiss While You're Dancing* (1934).

Eddy Duchin was born in Cambridge, Massachusetts, in 1909. Discovering his natural talent for the piano at a young age, he joined the Leo Reisman Orchestra in 1929. Thanks to his good looks as much as his talent, he soon became one of the country's most sought-after young bandleaders, repeatedly billed as "the Adonis of the supper club maestros." Needless to say, he was a hit with Persian Room audiences.

Sadly, Eddy died young, at the age of forty-one, from leukemia. But he packed a lot of living into the years he had. By 1934 he had developed a national following for his performances on radio shows and in 1936 was featured on *The Burns and Allen Show*. During that same time frame he was in a few movies—*Coronado* (1935) and *Hit Parade of 1937*—all while appearing at the Persian Room.

Eddy's son, Peter, continued in his fathers footsteps, taking up the baton with the Peter Duchin Orchestra. And yes, he also made a splash at the Persian Room, playing there for New Year's Eve in 1973 and '74.

Some other Persian Room performers from the 1930s:

Eve Becke
The Ray Benson
　Orchestra
The Emil Coleman
　Orchestra
Dario and Diane
Paul Draper
The Hartmans
The Henry King
　Orchestra

Lydia and Jareaco
Mario and Florio
Maurine and Norva
Pancho's Orchestra
Jane Pickens
Ramon and Rosita
George Sterney
Eve Symington

CHAPTER TWO

The 1940s

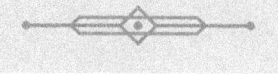

A 1945 magazine ad touting the "Incomparable" Hildegarde, nightly at the Persian at 9:30 and 12:30, except for Tuesday evenings when the pianist/chanteuse aired her weekly radio show.

It was in the '40s that American women entered the workplace in a major way, filling thousands of jobs vacated by men going off to war. Rosie the Riveter became a symbol of patriotism and can-do spirit for a new generation of empowered women. When, to everyone's joy, the war ended, those women went back to their homes and families—but they weren't the same. They'd had a taste of independence, and there would be no going back—not completely.

Radio was the main source of entertainment as well as information, bringing music, soap operas, game shows, and comedies, as well as news and sports, into living rooms across the country. Television had been introduced at the 1939 World's Fair, but it wasn't available to consumers until 1947. Even then, programming was extremely limited, and only a few privileged families owned one.

Fashions were austere in the early '40s because the War Production Board set strict limits on the amount of fabric allowed in the construction of garments. American designers compensated for cloth rationing by creating a new style of women's suits: short skirts topped by petite jackets. Nylon stockings were outlawed, forcing fashion-conscious ladies to draw simulated stocking seams down the backs of their legs with eyebrow pencils. New York designers, cut off from Paris couture, began to create new, peculiarly American garments—leisure outfits and less-constructed fashions that emphasized comfort and suited a more active, less formal lifestyle. Soon, the United States was the sportswear capital of the world.

In music, it was the era of the big bands and the exuberant dance known as the jitterbug. The most popular singers, including Bing Crosby, Dinah Shore, Perry Como, and Frank Sinatra, sang with the big bands before embarking on solo careers. John Birks "Dizzy" Gillespie introduced the generation to the sinewy, rebellious sounds of bebop and modern jazz. In baseball, Jackie Robinson led the Brooklyn Dodgers to six World Series.

Frozen dinners, computers, the bra, Tupperware, Dr. Spock, microwave ovens, the atom bomb, Slinkies, the Zoot Suit, aluminum foil, radar, penicillin, and pin-up girls all came to prominence in the 1940s. Humphrey Bogart, Jimmy Stewart, Joan Crawford, Bette Davis, Cary Grant, Doris Day, and hundreds of other stars were idolized for their larger-than-life glamour and for the ageless films they brought to life. As a repercussion of World War II, many European artists immigrated to the United States, and the nucleus of the art world swung from Paris to New York.

It won't surprise you to learn, however, that life in the Persian Room of the '40s held itself aloof from the harsher realities of the decade. Not unlike the escapist fare gracing movie screens about town, it provided those fortunate enough to afford a table an elegant refuge from the events of the day, though, when it came to raising money for war bonds, the Persian Room certainly did its part. And it offered a respite to the performers, too, many of whom had spent time overseas entertaining the troops and boosting morale.

Who better to start with, when evoking New York's finest night spot in the '40s, than Marge Champion? A prodigious legend who was nimble, vital, and constantly on the go up until the day we lost her in 2020 at age 101, she and her husband Gower were regulars at the Persian throughout the decade, with a devoted following. She was all too happy to reminisce—and her memory for the glorious details couldn't have been sharper.

. . . .

THE FIRST THOUGHT that popped into my head upon meeting Marge in the New York apartment that she's occupied for thirty-seven years was that the research from Quin, one of my trusty assistants, was faulty. No way this beautiful woman was ninety-two. But she is. I was invited to her home the day after she returned from Los Angeles, where she participated in something called *Christmas with Walt Disney* at the Walt Disney Family Museum. She actually pulled a muscle doing one of her high kicks there, recreating one of the routines she'd performed as a model for *Snow White* many decades earlier. Yes, high kicks!

"It seems as if you're out and about an awful lot, going to dance exhibits and all the Disney events," I commented. "Are you ever going to slow down?"

"You're right. I thought I'd be able to finally read some of the books on my shelves that I've never gotten to, but I'm so busy with all the appearances and requests I get! It's a definite blessing. I still take classes downstairs in the gym. There are a couple of gals who teach them that are wonderful, and I enjoy it because it sure keeps me going."

Marge was dancing almost as soon as she could walk, thanks to her father, Ernest Belcher. Ernest was the first dance director for motion pictures, and Marge told me that he'd worked with most of the top movie stars of the day, including Charlie Chaplin, Mary Pickford, Mack Sennett, Fred Astaire, Mae Murray, Shirley Temple, and John Gilbert.

By the time Marge was twelve, she was her father's assistant and demonstrator. "He'd call me in and ask me to show Tula Ellice Finklea [later known as Cyd Charisse] how a certain step or dance was done," she told me.

In the late 1930s and early '40s, Marge worked for Disney Studios as the moving model for Snow White, *Pinocchio*'s

Blue Fairy, Hyacinth Hippo in *Fantastia*, and numerous other characters that decades of children still love. Though she played small roles in such films as *Honor of the West*, *Sorority House*, and *The Story of Vernon and Irene Castle*, stage work was her bread and butter. She appeared in *Portrait of a Lady*, *Beggar's Holiday*, *The Little Dog Laughed*, and many other plays over her long career.

I have to interrupt Marge's story for a minute to tell you about her husband and dancing partner of thirty years, Gower Champion. Gower was only fourteen when he and his friend Jeanne Tyler entered and won the Veloz and Yolanda Waltz to Fame dance contest. A week's booking at the Coconut Grove was the prize. With his mother, Beatrice along to chaperone and help oversee negotiations, Gower and Jeanne, billed as "America's Youngest Dance Team," hit the road. They were successful not only in top-drawer New York nightclubs, but also landed featured dance roles in Broadway musicals such as *Streets of Paris* and *Count Me In*.

America's Youngest Dance Team broke up when Gower joined the Coast Guard during World War II.

"When Gower got out of the service he never wanted to be part of a dance team again," Marge told me. "He got a studio on the East Side of New York in an old church, with a huge room where he could choreograph and do things like that. Well, unfortunately, things didn't go exactly as he planned, and he had to become part of a team again."

When he tried to recruit Jeanne and resurrect their old act, he found her married and uninterested in picking up

MGM movie stars Marge and Gower Champion delighted patrons with their musical comedy hoofing and unparalleled ballroom dance elegance from 1947 to 1953 with their annual engagement at the Persian.

where America's Youngest Dance Team had left off. So in 1945 he went to Ernest Belcher, his former dance instructor, for advice. Ernest said, "Ask my daughter Marge; maybe she'd be interested." Clearly her interest went further than just dancing, and the feeling was mutual. They married on October 5, 1947.

"Right after Gower and I got married, we flew East and did a show with Milton Berle for television, which, in those days, practically no one saw because there just weren't that many TV sets. At the end of that week, we opened for Liberace at the Persian Room.

"For some strange reason—because Lee rarely got a bad review—we got better notices than he did. So Mame Abbott, who booked our engagement there, booked us again a year later, on our first wedding anniversary. This time we topped the bill, and that was very satisfying."

In their Persian Room engagements, Marge and Gower didn't just perform for politely seated spectators; they led the diners in the latest ballroom and swing dances with their own unique twist, making even the tango, waltz, and mambo look easy. "My father trained me as a ballet dancer," Marge explained, "and Gower taught me the other styles. New dances and steps were always being introduced."

"We were certainly never just a dance team. Our act was more like a musical revue— mostly dancing. We sang and talked and joked, all things that dance teams didn't generally do.

"There wasn't another room like the Persian Room, and because it was such an intimate space, it was friendly to us. We could talk to each other or directly to someone in the audience. Supper club audiences differ from stage audiences. You perform *for* stage audiences, but in supper clubs like the Persian Room, you have to make real contact with your audience or you don't get far.

"My father taught me there was a reason behind every movement. At the end of a number you don't just put out your hands. You have to think, 'There you are.' I think that's why we captured people. Gower never extended his hand to me just to swing me around. He always *gave me his hand*. There's a difference. David Craig, Nancy Walker's husband, used to teach that. Subtext.

"We came back on our sixth anniversary in 1953. By that time we had the Cheerleaders with us. They sang an opening number and introduced us through the lyrics of the song. They also occupied audiences while we made quick wardrobe changes. They'd sing, and I'd change in the kitchen.

"One of the big treats of performing there was that you got to stay at the Plaza for the run of your show—though they put us up in what used to be the maids' quarters, on the top floors. Going up to the room to change was out of the question, of course."

When the Plaza converted some of the units to condominiums in 2007, those maids' quarters were sold as penthouses and commanded prices starting at twenty million dollars. Sine then they have skyrocketed even higher!

During the 1950s, the Champions made Hollywood their home and turned most of their energy to film work. They appeared in Paramount's *Mr. Music* with Bing Crosby, the 1951 MGM revival of the musical *Show Boat*, *Everything I Have is Yours* (1952), and *Give a Girl a Break* (1953). In 1957 *The Marge and Gower Champion Show* on CBS shadowed their own story as they played two dancers trying to get out of show business.

They found fame on Broadway in the 1960s, choreographing and winning awards for such hits as *Bye, Bye Birdie* in 1961, *Hello Dolly* in 1964, and *I Do! I Do!* in 1966. The Champions divorced in 1973, and Gower continued his successful career on Broadway, passing away just hours before winning an Oscar for *42nd Street*. Well into her nineties, Marge remained sharp as a razor, traveling, giving lectures and talks, and occasionally performing. She may have lasted a few decades longer than the Persian Room itself, but she certainly cherished her memories of the place, just as we cherish our memories of *her*.

· · · ·

AS I MENTIONED, though the Plaza remained a bastion of elegance, it did its part in the war effort by raising literally millions in war bond sales. "The bigger the bond, the better the view" was the mantra for war bond fashion shows and auctions. And what was the reward for buying a hefty $1,000 bond? Ringside seats at a Persian Room performance by "the incomparable Hildegarde," by far the most beloved chanteuse of her day. At one show, a Hildegarde rendition of "The Last Time I Saw Paris" inspired a well-heeled fan to swell the coffers of the war effort to the tune of $25,000.

With her first performance there, at a Soldiers' and Sailors' Club benefit on September 23, 1941, Hildegarde (born Hildegarde Loretta Sell in Adell, Wisconsin, in 1906) changed the Persian Room forever. Eleanor Roosevelt called her "the first lady of supper clubs," and she was described waggishly by gossip columnist Walter Winchell as "the dear that made Milwaukee famous." No stranger to fame himself, Liberace described Hildegarde as "perhaps the most famous supper club entertainer who ever lived," while no less a personage than King Gustavus V of Sweden dubbed her "the girl with the eternal touch of Spring." But to all who loved her, she will always be known by the indelible moniker ascribed to Winchell: the Incomparable Hildegarde!

Hildegarde was a sultry, sophisticated singer, regal yet somehow approachable and funny. She was renowned for wearing chic over-the-elbow gloves, even when playing the piano, a signature that resulted from the time an orchestra leader inadvertently skipped her lead-in and she had no time to remove them. In an instant, she discovered she was comfortable playing with them on, and the rest was history. She wielded lace handkerchiefs flirtatiously and bestowed roses on her audience at the close of each show.

Sadly, I never had an opportunity to meet Hildegarde—she passed away quietly in a New York City hospital at the age of ninety-nine in 2005. But over a luscious steak dinner in the Plaza's Oak Room, Don Dellair, Hildegarde's last manager,

An ad for the Incomparable Hildegarde, who was called "the first lady of supper clubs" by no less an expert than Eleanor Roosevelt

reminisced and told me story after story about her.

"It was Hildegarde who made the Persian Room, and the Persian Room that made Hildegarde," he said. "I wasn't Hildegarde's manager when she began, I was just a teenager. Her manager then was Anna Sosenko, and Anna was something else. It all began when Hildy was performing across the street, at the Savoy Plaza. Anna came here to speak to the people at the Plaza about her. She said, 'She sings, she plays piano, she is witty, funny, and glamorous. She wears gorgeous stuff, and you should try her here at the Persian Room!' And that was how it all started.

"When Hildy played here, she did more weeks than anyone else. Everyone else got four weeks; Hildy got six months. Her favorite color was pink, and before they opened for a new season, the entire Persian Room was painted pink for Hildegarde. She literally put the Persian Room on the map: People started writing about it and saying things about it, like, 'They've painted the room. . . . Hildegarde must be coming!'

"Prior to her, they didn't really have headliners; they had a lot of great orchestras and wonderful dance teams, but Hildegarde was the first headliner. The Persian Room became famous because of Hildy's appearances there—but at the same time, Hildy became a household name because of the Persian Room.

"I want to talk about Anna for a moment," Don said as he pushed his very clean plate away, leaned back, and stretched, "because she was very much a part of this story, too. Anna was a great manager but very controlling. You want someone like that working for you. Anna insisted on working the lighting for Hildy's shows, and she once turned them out in the middle of Hildy's performance. I wasn't there, but I've heard the story many times. Apparently, Hildy didn't do something Anna had told her to do, so Anna just blacked out the lights and walked away!

"Always the trouper, Hildy didn't miss a beat. 'Oh, Alex,' she called, 'Alextrician!' That got a big laugh from the audience, who naturally thought it was part of the act, so she started using it all the time. Anna eventually came back and turned the lights back on. She was brilliant, but you had to do what she said. Hildegarde didn't mind a bit because she was a performer and just wanted to perform. She didn't want to worry or even think about the business side of things."

Although the Persian Room was her artistic home, Hildegarde performed in other clubs and on celebrated stages around the world. In addition to entertaining the likes of King Gustavus V of Sweden, King George V, and King George VI, she performed at the White House during both the Truman and Eisenhower presidencies.

Hildegarde's signature songs, " Darling, Je Vous Aime Beaucoup" and "The Last Time I Saw Paris," mesmerized audiences night after night, month after month, year after year. Broadway and Hollywood stars, denizens of high society, politicians, and heads of state attended Hildegarde's performances from 1941 through 1947. Though her regular annual engagements ended at that point, she returned to the Persian Room on and off until 1975. She was the highest paid supper club entertainer during 1944 and 1945, earning $2,000 to $3,000 per four-week engagement—in addition to a percentage of the house. Considering the fact that her shows were nearly always sold out, it amounted to quite a salary.

Don mesmerized me with his stories, but it wasn't until dessert that I was able to extract from him a personal memory of one of his first visits to the Persian Room.

"I was in college at this point, and two friends and I wanted to impress our girlfriends. So we decided to take them to the Persian Room to see the incomparable Hildegarde.

When we told the girls we were going, they were so excited they became giddy. Little did they know that once we got there we still had to stand in line—and one's place in line didn't matter. We were at the front of the line, but all the important people were ushered in ahead of us.

"Luckily, a very nice lady stood up for us, saying it was disgraceful that we had been waiting so long and demanding to speak to the person in charge. This was a very important woman (though I have no idea to this day who she was), and

Hildegarde was so swanky, she played the piano while wearing her opera gloves.

the head honcho came out and told us to come right in. Well, we might have been better off if we hadn't gotten in. Because when the bill came I looked at it and thought, 'Uh oh! I don't think we have enough.' We had no clue how expensive it would be. We should have known, but we just didn't think about it. At that point, the girls went to the ladies' room and told us to come get them when we had it figured out.

"The maître d' came over and asked us how much we had. We told him and gave it all to him, but it wasn't enough. The dinners were ten dollars each, which was a lot for us. Plus, the cover charge was two dollars a person. He asked us what we thought we should do. And we said we'd give him what we had, go home to Brooklyn, talk to our fathers, and come back later in the week with the balance of what we owed him. The man was so caring that he asked us how we were going to get home because we were giving him all our money. We said we'd take the subway, but he gave us enough money to take the girls home in a cab. He acted like a dad to us. But that was the Persian Room.

"Of course we brought back the money, and when we did, we asked to see the maître d'. 'Wow, you actually came back,' he said. 'I had a feeling you would!'"

Now that's a Persian Room story—because it's elegant. Everything about the Persian Room was like that.

. . . .

LIBERACE INITIALLY PLAYED the Persian Room in 1940, as an intermission pianist for thirty-five dollars a week. He didn't return as a headliner until seven years later, on October 12, 1947. And, with the characteristic extravagance that set him apart from all other performers, he brought with him a mind-blowing piano custom built by Julius Bluthner and promoted as the world's largest concert grand. Because of an inconvenient transportation strike in progress, the piano was delivered to the Plaza just in time for Liberace's magnificent entrance, which included the lighting of his candelabra, on display at the Plaza for the first time. He never did a performance without it after that.

Liberace was a remarkably accomplished concert pianist and a consummate showman, telling jokes and engaging the audience by asking for requests and improvising. At one point in his show he canvassed for help and brought a female volunteer up to sit next to him at the piano and assist him in a complicated classical arrangement. Her contribution consisted of hitting one single note on cue.

It was always a party with Liberace at the keyboard (even before he adopted his signature candelabra).

Liberace's great talent and friendly, humorous, exquisitely produced show whipped the audience into a frenzy. His outrageous wardrobe, featuring sequins, furs, and satins galore, was topped off by jewelry that looked too heavy for a mere human to wear. It almost always included a diamond-and-platinum ring shaped like a miniature piano. As for his personal attributes, *Variety* proclaimed, "Liberace looks like a cross between Cary Grant and Robert Alda." That was a compliment, by the way.

In looking for some personal Liberace stories, I turned once again to Don Dellair, as I knew they'd been good friends since Don's days as a member of the Tommy Wonder and Don Dellair dancing and singing team. (He later retired from performing and started the Don Dellair and Tommy Wonder Management Company.) This time, Don was to meet me at my apartment and pay the necessary attention to Sabrina and Marina, and then we'd head out for dinner. While we sat in my living room, I asked him if he really knew *everyone* from a certain era—or if it just seemed that way.

· · · ·

"WHEN YOU ARE lucky enough to get to a certain age, as I am, you know people," he responded.

"And you knew Liberace," I said, hoping he'd settle into the subject.

"Yes, he was a friend. A dear, dear soul. No matter what trouble he got into, he was the kindest, most gracious, angel of a person. He knew Hildegarde, you know," Don continued. "It was Tommy and I who introduced them. They were from the same city—Milwaukee. We introduced Hildy to Liberace because they were both our dear friends, and we knew they'd hit it off.

"Liberace's full name was Wladziu Liberace, and I don't know if Hildy told him to do it or if he did it because it worked for her, but he quickly dropped his first name and became known—well-known—as Liberace, although all his friends called him Lee.

Once, during her show at the Persian Room, Hildy introduced him to the audience. They gave him a very welcoming cheer, and Hildy said, 'I'm from Milwaukee; he has to be from Milwaukee. I am known by one name; he uses one name. I play the piano; he plays the piano; in fact, he copied my whole act.'"

"Liberace quickly quipped back, 'But I'm sure I have a few more gowns than you have, darling!' The audience howled. It was a thing of love with those two. Hildegarde introduced the song 'I'll be Seeing You,' and eventually Liberace became very well-known for singing that song."

When I visited with Marge Champion, she told me that she remembers a time before she and Gower became headliners, when they opened for Lee [as she called him]. She said he was always painting—many times something for her—and had an easel set up in his Plaza suite. " He also always requested a room with a long hallway so he could line up his suede shoes of various colors."

Marge smiled remembering those early years. " We were still in our twenties. He was the star of the show and had premature white hair with streaks. He used to send me to the drug store to get this black hair dye because he didn't want to be seen buying it. I sure got funny looks from the sales ladies because here I was, this young girl with blond hair, buying black hair color!"

"He was a swell guy. We were good friends with both him and his brother, who was also his manager."

It probably won't surprise you to learn that Don and I never did make it out to dinner that night. His stories just kept coming, and three hours later we were still sitting on my couch with the kids asleep on our laps. I would gladly forgo dinner any day of the week to listen to more.

. . . .

I THANK MY lucky stars that I had a chance to spend time with Celeste Holm just a year before her death in 2012, at the impressive age of ninety-five. There was certainly no hint of her mortality when I met her; in fact, she was downright lively.

Immediately upon entering Celeste's palatial Central Park West apartment I was awed her baby grand piano, situated with a commanding view of the park. But I was more impressed by the diminutive golden man perched on top of it—Celeste's Oscar for her Academy Award–winning performance in *Gentlemen's Agreement.* Although I've seen a few of the much-coveted statuettes over the years, this was my first opportunity to hold one, and it was intoxicating.

I was equally as thrilled to meet the lady herself, whose dazzling crystal-blue eyes flashed mischievous sparks as she spoke of years past with an absolute clarity that belied her age.

Celeste and her husband, opera singer Frank Basile, had invited me to visit them and talk about her experiences at the Persian Room in the '40s and '50s. But, before we fell headlong into the past, I had to satisfy my curiosity about the present. I asked Celeste, "What have you been up to lately?"

Frank jumped in, telling me proudly, "We were in Indiana just three weeks ago. I was giving a concert with the Indianapolis Opera. Celeste got up and did the last number with me and was brilliant, and the reviews said . . . 'Frank who? Celeste Holm holds court'!"

"What was the last number?" I asked.

"'Getting to Know You' from *The King and I*. Not a dry eye in the house while she sang it. I introduced her, saying, 'I'd like to welcome to the stage the legendary, the one and only Celeste Holm.' So, she came out on stage, and I started in, 'Celeste, you know, "It's a very ancient saying—"'"

At this point, Celeste chimed in, finishing the story—and the opening lyric: "As a teacher I've been learning, / you'll forgive me if I boast, / And I've now become an expert on the subject I like most / Getting to know you / getting to know all about you. . . . "

Celeste was born in New York, though she traveled extensively throughout her childhood (her father was an

The eternally elegant Celeste Holm.

insurance adjuster for Lloyd's of London) and attended schools in Europe as well as the United States. She was taking me through her background when Frank explained, "Celeste grew up with her parents in Chicago, but she never went to the University of Chicago."

"No, I never went to a university at all," she added, "although all of my biographies say I studied drama there. In fact, I was in high school and the principal suggested I take an advanced course in English offered by the University of Chicago, and I did. I think the university probably decided to take credit for me once I'd become successful. I never had any theatrical training at all, until much later."

"Later," Frank said, "was after she had an Oscar and three Academy Award nominations. That was when Elia Kazan suggested the Actor's Studio."

"After high school I came to New York and beat the pavement like everyone else."

In 1936 Celeste began her stage career, appearing as an ingénue in a stock production in Pennsylvania. That was followed by an offer to travel as the understudy for Ophelia in a production of *Hamlet* starring Leslie Howard. In 1938, Celeste made her New York stage debut in a small part in the short-lived comedy *Gloriana*.

In 1939, she landed her first starring role on Broadway in *The Time of Your Life*, co-starring with another theater newbie, Gene Kelly. Other parts followed, but it was in 1943 that Celeste became a star—singing the naughty (for its day) "I Can't Say No" as Ado Annie in *Oklahoma*. She'd been playing the role for just a few months when she took her first bow at the Persian Room.

"Celeste, how did you do fit it all in?" I asked. "I know your show didn't end until almost 11 p.m., and then you went on at the Plaza?"

"Well, I only had to be in *one* place at any given time, I guess. The curtain would come down and I'd run over to the Persian Room. Other entertainers went out and ate or socialized after their shows. I sang."

"I know, but the energy it took."

"In 1943 I was young, you know!"

Frank proudly chimed in, "The midnight show was the hottest ticket in town after hours, and the reviews . . . they said the Persian Room was *the* place to go."

He continued, "It was only a year after *Oklahoma*, in 1944, that John C. Wilson created *Bloomer Girl* specifically for Celeste, with her name over the title. She was the toast of the town—she was the toast of Broadway!"

It probably sounds as if Frank was right there with Celeste from the beginning, when actually he didn't enter the scene until 1990. But he made up for lost time by diligently organizing, chronicling, and archiving even the smallest details of Celeste's career.

"I just wanted to know my wife, so from the start I listened to her family and their stories, and we talked everyday about everything. As I go through and try to organize all her letters, notices, reviews, and other material—and we have a storage unit full—I'll ask about this and that. Over the years we've both enjoyed it. Celeste relives all the excitement, and I hear all these wonderful stories."

Following that success, Celeste gave in to Hollywood. In 1946, she signed a contract with Twentieth Century-Fox.

In spite of her defection to the West Coast, though, she continued to appear at the Persian Room when she could fit it into her schedule. "I was working and living at the Plaza late in the '40s—maybe 1949—with my young son Dan. He was the male version of Eloise."

I asked what Persian Room memories stood out above all others. She thought a bit, and then the lightbulb went off. "One very exciting incident occurred right around 1943. I actually helped the FBI apprehend some criminals!"

"Oh my God, yes," remembered Frank. "That's a major story. It really should be kept for Celeste's memoirs," he said—before continuing headlong into the tale. "Celeste had been introduced to some people when she was about ten years old in Paris with her parents. Fast-forward sixteen years to 1943 or '44, and she's in a hit musical, and the couple is in New York—passing bad checks around! They are telling people that they are friends of Celeste Holm's, using her name as collateral or a reference."

Celeste picked it up from there: "The FBI approached me and asked if I knew these people, to which I replied, no, not really. They told me what was going on, and I said, well, they've contacted me and it happens that I know where they will be tomorrow night. They'll be at my show at the Persian Room. They had asked me for tickets! Of course the FBI was very excited. We'll be there, the guys said, and if you just point them out to us, we'll arrest them."

Frank's turn: "Celeste carefully chose a certain red dress so that if any blood was spilt, it wouldn't show!"

Was any blood spilled? I had to know.

"No," said Celeste. "The bad guys came in and sat down and I started my show, but the FBI didn't arrive for the longest time. Don't forget, this was the late show. I tried to think what I should do, so I keep ad-libbing and stalling and all kinds of stuff to keep the show going."

Frank jumps in, "Finally, they show up, and Celeste dramatically points them out from the stage. The FBI men arrest them and the next day the papers have headlines saying: Celeste Holm, Finger Woman!!"

Persian Room patrons got a great encore that night.

It might not be as edge-of-your-seat exciting as helping to apprehended criminals, but I did want to know some particulars about Celeste's act.

Did you sing all the great songs from *Oklahoma*?

"Oh no, I couldn't do that. I wasn't allowed to do it. When

you are in a current Broadway show they won't let you sing those songs anywhere else. But I had songs written just for me to sing at the Persian Room."

"'Eunice from Tunis' was written just for her," Frank added. "In fact, *Life* magazine did a whole spread of Celeste and her photos and faces for 'Eunice.'"

At that point, Frank looked as if he had just remembered something. "Honey," Frank led Celeste, "everyone came to see you at the Persian Room. Do you remember?"

"Oh, of course I remember. I bet you're thinking of the Duke of Windsor and Mrs. Simpson."

"That's right," said Frank. "They got to know Celeste when she was in *Oklahoma*. They would always visit backstage, and they came to see her at the Persian Room all the time, because they lived at the Plaza. In fact, when the Duke was dying, he asked to see Celeste. She went to entertain him in his last week. And John Kennedy knew you when you were in *Oklahoma*, that's way before he was a senator." He turned to me at that point and said, "They dated, you know."

"You and JFK?" I asked her.

"We went on a few dates," she admitted.

When I was going through some of the many books and papers from Celeste's career, I came across a touching letter written to Celeste from a group of servicemen who said that they had seen *Oklahoma* twice and heard her sing "Eunice from Tunis" at the Persian Room. "The soldiers came to see her religiously," Frank told me.

I found another heartwarming letter from a man, now a grandfather, who was coming to New York. He wanted Celeste to know that he remembered sitting under a tree in 1946, in occupied and later reclaimed France, when a Jeep came by and a young lady took time from her schedule to make him and his two friends feel like they were home. He had made it back, gotten married, and now had grandchildren, and he often brought them to New York and regaled them with the memory of that day.

It was at Twentieth Century-Fox that Celeste made the first nine movies of her career—and what formidable movies they were. She took home the Oscar in 1947 and went on to play numerous touching and comedic roles. A highlight was her turn as a mental patient in *Snake Pit* (1948), the first film to depict the dark side of mental illness.

Celeste was nominated twice more, for Best Supporting Actress for *Come to the Stable* (1949), in which she played a tennis-playing French nun trying to build a children's hospital—seriously—and in *All About Eve* (1950) with Bette Davis. After completing that film, Celeste decided that she missed performing for a live audience and surprised the industry by buying out the remainder of her Fox contract and heading back to Broadway.

In the '50s, Celeste was enticed back to Hollywood, and she had a chance to showcase her lighter side with musical roles in *The Tender Trap* (1955) with Debbie Reynolds and *High Society* (1956) with Grace Kelly and Bing Crosby. Both costarred Frank Sinatra.

During the next four decades, Celeste kept the airlines in business, traveling between Hollywood and Broadway as well as singing at prestigious clubs including the Persian Room. The reviews of her 1958 Persian Room appearance were as impressive as those from 1943.

Celeste and Frank were such wonderful hosts that before I knew it, four hours had flown by. We made plans to get together again, but before I left, the romantic in me had to find out how this great and still affectionate couple had met.

"It was fate. We were introduced but had actually met two years earlier. And I think Celeste thought I was . . . hmmm, what did you say?"

"I said you were a very beautiful man."

"I think you said the most beautiful man you had ever seen." Frank twinkled, and he continued, "Actually the formal introduction came about because I was in New York and was asked to sing at a big charity gala in New Jersey, and Celeste was one of the guests. Her ride home had to leave early and asked me if I would drive her home. Of course, I said yes, I would be honored. After I did my part of the show, she asked me if I wanted to sit and eat at her table. So I sat down, and we talked. It was a wonderful evening. We danced and then talked all the way home, and just as I was approaching Manhattan, she said 'Oh, no—I'm going to my farm,' which was two hours in the other direction!

"I had a girlfriend at the time, a relationship that I was sorting out. But once I did, I spent all my time with Celeste. We hit it off so quickly as best friends that I was afraid to tell her that I was in love with her. It turned out she was feeling the same. She said I probably don't have much time left in the world, but if I can borrow you for three years. . . . "

I couldn't help exclaiming, "What a love story!"

"That's what she says! And you know, it's been eleven years."

Celeste and Frank were married on Celeste's eighty-fifth birthday, when Frank was forty-seven, making her one of the original cougars! Good for her. Good for them.

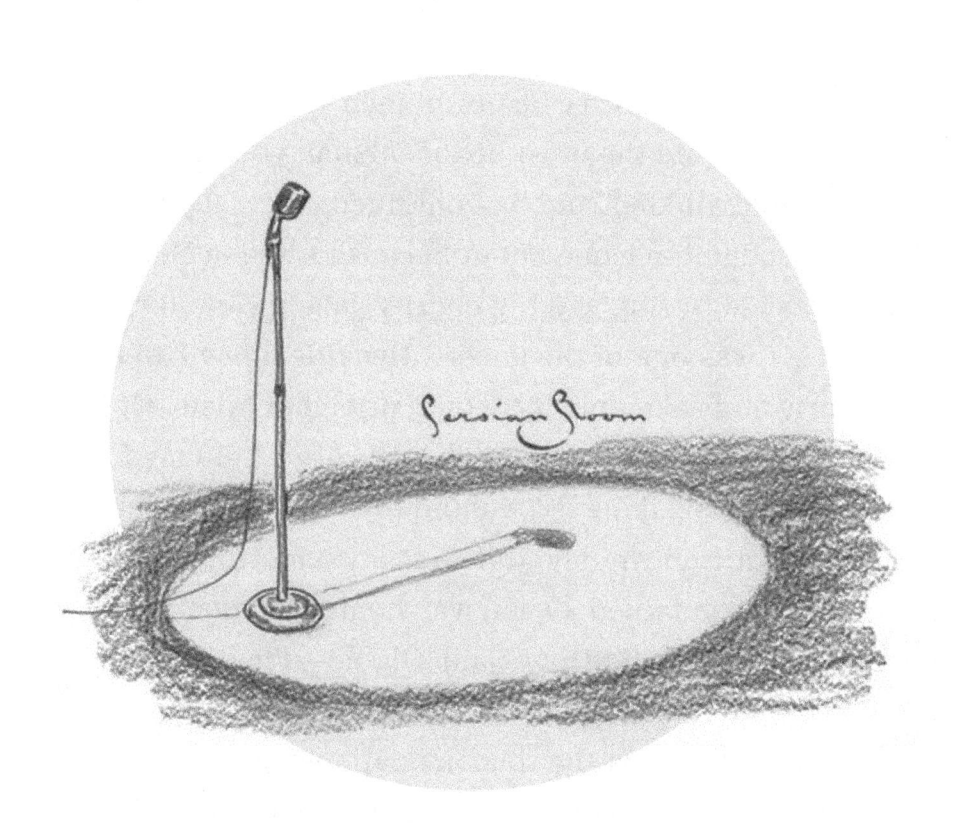

. . . .

Some other Persian Room performers from the 1940s:

Fred and Elaine Barry
Victor Borge
Carol Bruce
John Buckmaster
Columbus and Carroll
Ben Cutler's Orchestra
Sally and Tony De Marco
Carmen Rivero
Jayne and Adam DiGatano
Morton Downey
Dick Gasparre and His Orchestra
Bob Grant Orchestra
Paul Haakon
Josephine Houston
Laurette and Clyman
Leni Lynn
Maurice and Cordoba
Sara Ann McCabe
Susan Miller
Jacques Peals
Rolly Rolls
Rosario and Antonio
Larry Siry and His Orchestra
Ted Straeter and His Orchestra
Russell Swann
Jane Winton

CHAPTER THREE

The 1950s

A quiet Persian Room prior to opening.

The end of World War II brought thousands of young American men home, and with them came a renewed vitality and passion for fresh beginnings. Returning vets married their sweethearts and began to buy things, including homes outside large cities. *The suburbs* entered the American lexicon, and the baby boom was off to a rousing start.

The decade began as a conservative time: "Under God" was incorporated into the Pledge of Allegiance. Family dynamics and gender roles were precisely defined. Women were housewives; men, providers; and teenagers were expected to mind their elders. (The term *teenager* itself was coined in the '50s.) But there was no holding back social and moral evolution. Under the burgeoning influence of television, movies, radio, and popular magazines, teens developed their own unique style and the rebellious behavior to go with it.

It was the period of James Dean jackets and swagger, hula hoops, ducktails, drive-in movies, beehive hairdos, poodle skirts, saddle shoes, and blue jeans. In a more serious vein, the nascent civil rights movement, which gathered steam with the 1954 Supreme Court ruling in *Brown v. Board of Education*, was on its way to becoming a juggernaut, and those formerly complacent housewives began to question their lot and explore their options.

On the music scene, the conservatism of the '40s began to ebb with this new decade. At the dawn of the 1950s, the hub of the world's music industry was midtown Manhattan. It was there that the three principle music labels had their headquarters—Columbia, Decca, and RCA—and so did the majority of music publishers. Music was in the air! Nightclubs and supper clubs gently phased out exhibition dancing and big band orchestras, replacing them with headliners from all spheres of show business.

The 1950s gave birth to rock-and-roll. Elvis Presley exploded in popularity, bolstered by controversial appearances on *The Ed Sullivan Show* and *American Bandstand*, TV shows that brought up-to-the-moment records and artists into living rooms nationwide. But Sullivan served up plenty more than rock-and-roll on his show, which ran from 1948 to 1971. There was plenty of "grown-up" entertainment, too, including appearances by Liberace, Carol Channing, Sal Mineo, Jane Morgan, Johnnie Ray, Tony Bennett, and many others. Their televised performances inspired people to seek them out in person, at such venues as the Persian Room.

Songstress Toni Arden (born Antoinette Ardizzone) appeared at the Persian Room with brother Jan throughout the 1950s.

More than ever before, we were presented with diverse musical choices, introduced to different styles and sounds. Bill Haley had us rocking around the clock, while Elvis's unique style was so scandalous that when he appeared on TV, the camera could only show him from the waist up. And Chuck Berry . . . well Chuck introduced us to a crazy amalgam of blues, rock, and country all wrapped in one crazy package.

On the opposite side of the rock-and-roll coin were the clean-cut heartthrobs, dreamboats, and teen idols. Paul Anka was a "Lonely Boy" who begged us, "Put Your Head on My Shoulder"; Fabian was a "Tiger" begging to be turned loose; and Pat Boone wrote "Love Letters in the Sand" and promised "April Love." Their counterparts were a variety of girl singers that included Patti Page, Patsy Cline, Lesley Gore, Diahann Carroll, Kay Thompson, and many other greats.

We had choices. Country music grew in popularity after Sun Records in Memphis introduced us to the Million Dollar Quartet: Jerry Lee Lewis, Johnny Cash, Carl Perkins, and—oh yeah—Elvis.

In 1952, Sony's introduction of the transistor radio made music portable. The hits went everywhere we did! In the movies we saw Humphrey Bogart instruct Miss McCardell to "get reservations at the Persian Room" for him and Sabrina.

It was an affluent time in New York City. New, futuristic museums were inaugurated, Broadway theater thrived, and contemporary art galleries opened all over town. New York became the epicenter of the American cultural map and has remained so ever since.

So, what was going on at the Plaza? For starters, owner Conrad Hilton recruited designer Henry Dreyfuss to thoroughly revamp the Persian Room. The result was a clean, modern design in blues and greens. Metallic mesh drapes custom made by Dorothy Liebes and two striking screens embellished with a stunning gold-and-white diamond pattern added elegance. And, because no detail was ever overlooked at the night spot, contemporary china in a coordinating blue-and-green diamond pattern complemented the scheme. The estimated cost of the transformation was $200,000, and the revitalized Persian Room reopened with appropriate fanfare on September 28, 1950.

The swank hotel changed hands in 1955 when Hilton sold it to the Hotel Corporation of America, controlled by A. M. Sonnabend. For those of you interested, this was the same year that New York City installed its first three-color traffic signals.

I was fortunate enough to meet a number of the best performers to grace the Persian Room stage during the '50s, many of whom are still actively performing. They all agree that there is no modern-day equivalent to the place, especially in its newly decorated 1950s glory.

· · · ·

AT THE TIME of her death in 2015, at age 90, Julie Wilson had been an American icon and cabaret queen for sixty-five-plus years, celebrated for her dramatically naughty renderings of torch songs, her dazzling designer gowns topped by ostentatious feather boas, and that ubiquitous gardenia behind her left ear.

In 1951, after her show at the posh Mocambo nightclub in Hollywood, Julie met the composer Cole Porter. "Patricia Morison had told him he should consider putting me in *Kiss Me Kate* because Lisa Kirk was leaving," recounted Julie. "Well, the club manager brought him backstage after the show, and after he introduced us, Mr. Porter looked me up . . . and then looked me down . . . and didn't say anything for what seemed like a very long time. Then he said 'You'd make a lovely Bianca.' That was that. I got the part, replacing Lisa in the tour heading to London. I stayed on in England for a few years doing *South Pacific* and *Bells Are Ringing* after *Kiss Me Kate*. At the same time, I studied at the Royal Academy of Dramatic Arts.

"At a certain point, I was missing New York, and it was time to start thinking about going home. Luckily, my manager told me he had booked me to open the fall season at the Persian Room."

Arriving home Julie lived in two worlds: Broadway and supper clubs. After wowing the crowds at the Persian Room, she returned to the theater in *Kismet*, *Pajama Game*, and others including the 1988 musical *Legs Diamond*, in which she appeared with Peter Allen in a part he wrote just for her, singing a song—"The Music Went Out of My Life"–he wrote with her in mind. Although the play was a legendary flop, Julie receved a Tony Award nomination.

When Julie and I walked into Manhattan's legendary

*Was there ever a chanteuse more
sophisticated and sultry than Julie Wilson?*

Russian Tea Room, the lunch patrons might not have immediately recognized her, but there was no mistaking the fact that this svelte, reed-straight, elegant woman was "somebody." Maybe it was her eyes, which still twinkled mischievously, or the come-hither smile that could still turn the heads of men of all ages. I must admit feeling a bit intimidated myself by this meticulously styled and pulled-together, self-assured octogenarian in a fabulous hat.

I say we met for lunch, but show-business people keep their own schedules. "Even though it's 1 p.m., it's breakfast time for me," Julie pointed out. "After so many years of working till the early, early hours and then sleeping until the afternoon, rising late has become a habit."

Looking every bit the gently aging siren, Julie informed the waitress that she needed black coffee, right away.

"Are you still serving breakfast?" she asked.

"No, but how about vichyssoise? Cold soup?"

"My dear," Julie replied, delighted with the opening, "I like my men and my soup *hot*!"

I believe Mae West delivered a version of that line, but Julie's performance was uniquely her own, sweet yet haughty, accompanied by a coy flutter of eyelashes for maximum dramatic effect. The waitress paused, then gave a good hearty laugh, as if she couldn't believe the innuendo had come out of the mouth of the grande dame seated before her. She also knew she'd have a good story to tell later.

As soon as we were settled, I got Julie reminiscing about the Persian Room.

"I was wrapping up a show in England when I received word from my manager that I had an offer to open the season at the Persian Room. My English girlfriend from the show, Sally, thought it a grand reason for us to go shopping in Paris, and I had some beautiful couture gowns designed for me by Balmain. Fabulous gowns! The Persian Room was so unique," she continued. "It was a marvelous room, and Ted Straeter's Orchestra played 'The Most Beautiful Girl in the World' every night as I was introduced."

"Many, many great things happened during my engagement there, and I met a lot of wonderful people, but I had one experience that luckily never happened to me again. One night, right at ringside was a couple who had obviously been enjoying their drinks. I was singing my heart out, and the gentleman kept shouting, 'Play "Melancholy Baby"!' This went on all evening long. I told him sweetly that I didn't have the arrangements for that song, but he would not be quiet.

"I thought, my God, what do I do now? I've tried everything I can think of. I really tried to ignore him but he wouldn't stop yelling 'Play "Melancholy Baby"!'—and he was getting drunker and drunker. I thought that maybe if I fussed over him, he'd be satisfied, so I went to his table with my cord and mike and said, 'I'm sorry I can't play your favorite song, but I hope you are having a good time and enjoying your nice dinner anyway. What are you having?' And he said, 'I'll show you what I'm having!' and he tilted his plate toward me until—whoosh! His food just cascaded all over my gown! Steak, gravy, sweet potatoes—all over my dress. My beautiful Balmain *gown*!

"It was probably my own fault for talking to some drunk. Nothing like that has ever happened to me since. And you know what? It ended just as it would in the movies. A man got up from the table across the way and took one of the guy's arms and another man nearby, a large monster of a man, stood up and took his other arm, and they picked him up from his chair and threw him out of the Persian Room and into the marble foyer. With that, I went back to the mike and said, 'Thank you for being such a nice audience. I'm sorry for the disturbance,' and I finished my show.

The soigné Julie Wilson became the undisputed Queen of New York cabaret in the 1980s after a 15-year detour to care for her family in Nebraska.

"Then I went upstairs to my room and cried like a baby! I was so humiliated. The audience was really great, and some lovely man—actually the president of one of the big talent agencies—called me up the next day to congratulate me on my composure. That made everything alright. It had just been one of those nights. You can find scoundrels anywhere, and that night was my turn. I love performing, and the Persian Room was one of the very best places."

With that painful tale out of the way, Julie relaxed and told story after story.

"I used to check out the room in the early evening, before people were seated. It reminded me of a fairyland. Even when the place was empty, it was so magical. The small round tables were draped with double tablecloths, the first skirting the floor and the second artfully arranged over it. The magnificent floral centerpieces made the whole room smell like a garden, scented with roses or whatever was in season at the time. Interestingly, once the room filled with people, the air changed—it began to smell like money! I could smell the expensive, custom-made perfumes and pungent men's colognes from the stage."

Julie and I became friends, and wherever we'd go, from coffee shops to the Café Carlyle, she had the same electric effect on people that I witnessed the first time I met her. She performed at cabarets and clubs around the country, but she told me she derived particular pleasure and satisfaction from her participation in the International Cabaret Conference at Yale University. It was there, at "Cabaret Camp," as Julie called it, that she got a chance to meet, teach, inspire, and encourage the next generation of musical performers. It is honestly hard for me to believe that Julie is gone—but thankfully, her music—and her memories—live on.

. . . .

PRESIDENT REAGAN PROCLAIMED Andy Williams's voice a national treasure. I'm not about to challenge that assertion, but Andy wasn't always the suave solo crooner that most of us adored, who performed to sold-out audiences around the globe until shortly before his death in 2012.

At the tender age of eight, while in the third grade, Andy joined his three brothers singing in the church choir. They were an instant local hit and started to perform regularly on the radio in nearby Des Moines, Iowa, as the Williams Brothers Quartet. Bob, Don, Dick, and Andy were on a roll, and by 1944, they found themselves backing up Bing Crosby on his hit record "Swinging on a Star."

Soon, the Williams Brothers hit the road, touring the country with Kay Thompson, and it was with her, in 1951 and again in September 1952, that they performed at the Persian Room. Reviewers called the act "trendsetting."

When I spoke with Andy, the first thing I wanted to know was, what was so unusual about that "trendsetting" act.

"Well, first of all, we moved around! That probably doesn't sound so groundbreaking, but believe me, it was. Prior to us, nightclub entertainers had traditionally stood in one spot and performed. If there was more than one singer, you all clustered around the microphone the best you could."

"We actually had a choreographer—Bob Alton. So that we could move around more easily, we hung the mics from the ceiling, and I mean *we* hung the mics. We actually got up on ladders ourselves and put them where we wanted them, and then we were able to move all over the stage, making our act sort of like a mini musical revue.

"Kay was an enormously dynamic performer. The act she put together was very fast and sophisticated, with high energy and lots of dance movements and singing. Two of our signature numbers were 'It's a Jubilee Time' and 'Pauvre Suzette.' In 'Suzette,' Kay sang, and my brothers and I were at the four corners, harmonizing and dancing around her.

"We were all the same height and wore matching dark blue suits and ties, and, as the song was about the men in her life, Kay sang to each of us in turn, injecting different celebrities' names into the skit as her lovers. One she loved 'not enough,' one 'she loved too much,' another 'she loved too often,' and one 'she didn't love.' I was the one she 'loved too much.'

"When she was done singing to me, I fell to the floor, rolled on my back, and wiggled my feet in the air. It was quite a workout. At the end of the thirty-five-minute show, Kay, my brothers, and I—and the audience—felt like we had performed a full Broadway show."

"We all stayed at the Plaza for the duration of the run, and it was there in the lobby that I was introduced to Stanley Marcus—you know, the cofounder of the Neiman Marcus department stores? He suggested that I take advantage of all the art and culture New York City had to offer, that I should walk and explore and learn from its many galleries and museums. I took his advice and forged a deep appreciation and love for modern art."

That experience clearly set something in motion. Andy became a major art collector.

The Williams Brothers and Kay Thompson were booked to open the Persian Room again in September of 1953, but Kay cancelled the engagement. Their final appearance together was on July 23, 1953, in Lake Tahoe.

Soon after that, Andy embarked on a solo singing career and his brothers left to pursue their individual interests. In 1962, Andy was asked to sing the Johnny Mercer and Henry Mancini song "Moon River" at the Oscars, and it swiftly became his signature song. In his later years, he would own, manage, and perform at his own club in Branson, Missouri, dubbed the Moon River Theater.

Before he was world famous as a soloist, Andy Williams (far left) was a member of the Williams Brothers.

.   .   .   .

KAY THOMPSON MAY have parted ways with the Williams boys but she continued to perform, designing a one-woman act and presenting it at the Persian Room in January 1954 to mixed response. Unfazed by the reviews, Kay tweaked the act a bit, changing the format to a two-person show, with Paul Methuen playing straight man and butler to Kay's eccentric persona. Bingo—she was back at the Plaza in November of that same year.

Kay began her career as a vocal coach for radio in the 1930s and was a regular on *The Bing Crosby –Woodbury Hour* and *The Fred Waring–Ford Dealers Show*. Her big break came in 1943, when her good friend Hugh Martin enlisted in the army and recommended her as his replacement as head vocal arranger at MGM. It was there at MGM that Kay coached singers she would work with for the length of her career, including Judy Garland and Frank Sinatra. In 1948, she left MGM to develop her own nightclub act with the Williams Brothers. They made a striking team that surprised and thrilled audiences across the country until they disbanded in 1953.

At some point in her whirlwind of a life, Kay developed an alter ego. "I am Eloise. I am six," she'd coo, to explain away some transgression or other. "You're late, Kay," someone would complain, and she'd bat her eyes, adopt a wide stance, and purr, "I am Eloise. I am six!" She used the gambit so many times—in life and in her act—that it became a part of her, and when her friend Dee Dee Dickson suggested she write a book featuring the six-year-old scamp, well, the rest is history.

There's no talking about Kay Thompson and Eloise without talking about Hilary Knight, the celebrated illustrator best known for collaborating with her on the *Eloise* books. And even better than talking *about* him is talking *to* him. Hilary may never have played the Persian

The uniquely accomplished Kay Thompson first performed at the Persian Room in 1951 with the Williams Brothers, but soon brought her solo act there—including her imitation of a little girl she dreamed up named Eloise.

Room, but he certainly has warm memories of the multitude of times he sat in the audience. (And, of course, it is his portrait of Eloise that graces the Plaza lobby to this day.)

Hilary was a gift to me from Kaye Ballard. When I talked to Kaye, she said, "You must talk to Hilary. He knows everything." That led to a treasured friendship, and you know what? Kaye wasn't too far off. Hilary might not know everything, but this born-and-bred New Yorker knows a lot!

With his knack for setting the scene, Hilary suggested we meet in the Plaza's Champagne Court, the spot that was once the Persian Room. It was a superb idea—and not only for communing with the local ghosts; they also serve a fabulous brunch. Hilary ordered eggs Benedict and I had yogurt, berries, and a chocolate croissant—fruit cancels out chocolate, right?

Once we'd taken the edge off our appetites, I knew Hilary was ready to reminisce.

"I've been around a long time and always worked around show business and show people, so yes, I know a lot of people and have had a lot of adventures," he admitted.

I was eager to learn how he and Kay Thompson began working together, though I rightfully surmised he'd told the story many times. Very graciously, he started to answer me—but then he mentioned Lisa Kirk, the legendary star of *Kiss Me Kate* and other Broadway shows and a mainstay of the Persian Room. I guess we got a little bit sidetracked.

"Lisa Kirk! I gushed—did you see Lisa perform here?"

"Yes I did," he replied, "and I made some earrings for her. It was a hobby of mine when I was very young. I sold a lot of my jewelry at the American House, at Fifty-fourth and Madison, as well as a few other shops. I made quite a bit of money!

"Then I went into the service," he continued, clearly immersed in his own recollections while I absorbed them all quite happily. Plenty of time to get back to Kay Thompson later. "When I got out, I had decided to try drawing as a career, but along the way I met Lisa. She and Patricia Morison were starring in *Kiss Me Kate*, and Lisa saw something I had made for Patricia. She called me up and said she was doing this act and asked me to make her a pair of earrings."

At this point, we'd wandered a bit far afield, and I hoped to get Hilary back to his memories of the Persian Room. He obliged me by mentioning that his very first visit there was to see Hildegarde. "I was just a teenager," he was quick to point out. "It's interesting; I remember seeing Hildegarde, Lisa Kirk, and Kay Thompson here, but I can't tell you much about their acts."

Lounging in our plush velvet, high-backed chairs, looking out onto Fifth Avenue, nibbling croissants and talking about the elegant old days, I couldn't have passed a more enjoyable afternoon, though we still hadn't talked about how *Eloise* came to be. No matter; Hilary was working his way up to it in his own way.

"I lived right here on Fifty-second Street," he began. "If you threw a stone in a straight line, where it stopped would be my apartment. My neighbor, in 1954, was Dee Dee Ryan. She was a fashion girl at *Harper's Bazaar* under Mrs. Vreeland. She called herself the photo editor, but really she was a glorified assistant.

"At that point, my job was doing humorous drawings for *House & Garden* and *Gourmet*. My inspirations were British cartoonist Ronald Searle and a little British humor magazine called *Lilliput*. My sketches were particularly influenced by Ron's terrible little St. Trinian school girls. They were all these horribly ugly little girls in school uniforms, getting into dreadful trouble right under the headmistress's nose.

"Even before I met Kay, I would do drawings for Dee Dee and slip them under her door. They were just my way of saying hi. Other people leave notes; I left sketches. One time I did a drawing of this little, blond, curly-haired girl, and another day I left a sketch of a mean little dark-haired girl who carried a club. Eventually, I intermingled the two, and that was really the beginning of Eloise.

"Dee Dee and I used to get together after work and go someplace to eat. We liked a small inexpensive place called the Golden Pheasant and would go there a lot. Neither one of us had any money, but we loved to go out and talk about work. In the scope of her job, Dee Dee worked with the photographer Richard Avedon. Sometime around 1951, Avedon went out to California to shoot Kay Thompson, and Dee Dee went along. I had once made a white feather fan, and Dee Dee took it to California for the shoot. Well, Avedon's shot with the fan turned out to be a wonderful picture: a close-up of Kay holding the fan with one loose feather draped across her nose.

"It was at the photo shoot that Dee got to know Kay, and they kept in touch. Time went by, and when Kay was performing her act at the Persian Room, Dee went to see her. There was a part in her act where Kay did this whole bit speaking in a little-girl voice. After the show, Dee Dee rushed up to Kay and said, 'You have to write a book about that little girl character of yours—and I live next door to the perfect person to do the drawings!' She showed Kay a few of the drawings I had slipped under her door, and Kay said, 'Tell him to come to my show and we'll talk afterward.'

"So of course that is exactly what we did. Dee Dee and I came to the Persian Room, and I brought along my drawing portfolio. After the show, Dee introduced us, and we went to the Palm Court, where I showed Kay some of my work. We started working on our first book right away, and within a year, it was done.

"We worked side by side, right here at the Plaza. She'd give me little lines, like, 'I have a dog who looks like a cat,' and I'd draw. You know, she had an apartment here for a long time.

"Our first book, just called *Eloise*, came out in November of 1955. *Eloise in Paris* came out the following year. For that one, we went to Paris twice to soak up the atmosphere. Then came *Eloise's Christmas* and *Eloise in Moscow*, and finally we went to Rome for *Eloise Takes a Bawth*, which we worked on for four years. Oh, it was a magical time."

Eloise turned fifty-five in November 2010, and Hilary is still as enthralled with her as ever. He is constantly asked by bookstores to sign autographs and give talks on her. A few years ago, Hilary generously donated all of his writing and illustrations to the New York Public Library.

Perhaps you think we've wandered away from nightlife at the Persian Room, but the spirit of the Plaza in the '50s is present in every wonderful word and drawing of the Eloise books, so I'm sure you'll agree that it was a worthwhile detour. And since Eloise herself wasn't available for an interview (taking a *bawth*, no doubt), Hilary made a brilliant substitute.

I knew he'd have a lot to say about Kay Thompson, but his vivid memories of Lisa Kirk came as a wonderful surprise.

. . . .

LISA'S KIRK'S *EIGHT* appearances at the Persian Room were extraordinary but really weren't planned. Born in Brownsville, Pennsylvania, in 1925, she had been accepted and enrolled to study law at the University of Pittsburgh when she traveled to New York to keep a friend company as she auditioned for the chorus line at the Versailles nightclub. I don't

An ad for one of Lisa Kirk's eight Persian Room appearances. She has described her onstage persona as "a sextrovert without being a sintrovert."

know if her friend made the cut, but Lisa was offered a place in the line—the back row, but it was a start. College was forgotten, and law was traded for show business.

Lisa gradually migrated from the back row to singing with the band between shows. Soon she was winning small parts in Broadway musicals; the first being *Good Night, Ladies* in 1945. It was in the 1947 production of Rodgers and Hammerstein's *Allegro*, singing "The Gentleman is a Dope," that she became a real Broadway presence. The next year she had the lead role in Cole Porter's *Kiss Me Kate*. After a year and a half, she handed it off to none other than Julie Wilson.

During Lisa's eighth cabaret show at the Persian Room, she was flanked by four dancing and singing boys, billed as the Four Saints. MGM records was so enthusiastic about the show that, with the assistance of the popular musical director Don Pippin, it was recorded and released as *Lisa Kirk at the Plaza*.

Hilary spoke admiringly of Lisa. "She was a great performer, wonderful looking with a terrific voice. You know, when they made the movie of *Gypsy* with Rosalind Russell, it was Lisa's voice singing, not Rosalind's. And her husband, Bob Wells, wrote the 'Eloise' song for Kay."

In past interviews Lisa described her style as "sextrovert" without being a "sintrovert." "A sextrovert is a girl who's sexy, but not in an obviously naughty way. The minute you get obvious, you're being a 'sintrovert,' and that isn't good."

After her huge stage success in *Kiss Me Kate* in 1948, she spent forty years entertaining in the Persian Room and other nightclubs, on Broadway, and in films, including *Here's Love*; *Me Jack, You Jill*; Jerry Herman's *Mack and Mabel*; Mel Brooks's 1968 film *The Producers*; and Noël Coward's *Design for Living*.

Lisa passed away on November 11, 1990, at sixty-five, from lung cancer, although she didn't smoke. Some say it was all of that secondhand smoke she inhaled while entertaining in nightclubs, but we'll never know.

. . . .

LISA KIRK WASN'T the only performer recorded live at the Persian Room. The high-class supper club snapped to a new beat when jazz arrived in September 1958, in the form of Miles Davis, Billie Holiday, Jimmy Rushing, and Duke Ellington.

The aforementioned greats assembled at a party hosted by Columbia Records, and the recording of the event was not intended as anything more than a souvenir. But the sounds were too bracing, too edgy, too scorchingly hot *not* to share with the public. The party lasted into the early morning, and the result was not one but two albums. *The Miles Davis Sextet—Jazz at the Plaza* featured Miles Davis, John Coltrane, Julian Adderley, Bill Evans, Paul Chambers, and Jimmy Cobb. Duke Ellington, Billie Holiday, and Jimmy Rushing were showcased on *Duke Ellington and His Orchestra—Jazz at the Plaza*. Was it a new era for the Persian Room? Not really, but it was certainly a once-in-a-lifetime moment.

. . . .

SPEND TIME WITH before her death in 2014 was the great Polly Bergen. Before the reminiscing began, she patiently explained the nightclub scene hierarchy of the 1950s to me. "The Copa was the big, big star place to play. That's where Frank Sinatra played." (Frank also played the Persian Room, but we'll get to that further down the road.) "It was rather like Vegas East Coast: big draws, big money, in a very commercial hotel. There was the Empire Room in the Waldorf Astoria, but that was a terrible room, and people didn't like to play it.

"Then there was the Persian Room, and it was the most beautiful room to play in the world. The Plaza was a selective venue. It was almost square, and the orchestra and the stage—well, it really wasn't a stage but the area where we sang—was in one point of the square and when you sang you were looking out to the three other points. It was a totally clear, perfect place to play; you could see everyone, and they could see you. It was not small but still very intimate in the way it was placed."

Polly became a household name through her numerous and varied stage and television appearances. She costarred with Gregory Peck and Robert Mitchum in the very dramatic *Cape Fear* and again with Mitchum, almost twenty years later, in *The Winds of War* and *War and Rememberance* (garnering Emmy nominations in the process). My favorite Polly moments are her comedic turns in *Move Over, Darling*, with Doris Day and James Garner, and the 1964 *Kisses for My President*, where she portrayed the first female president of the United States. (We're all still waiting to see that happen for real.)

Although Polly has been recognized for her acting, when I asked her if she had to pick a favorite talent, she quickly replied that it was singing. She'd been singing, on radio and in small venues from the age of fourteen, and that had opened doors to acting.

A few years later, and after studying math in community college, Polly attracted the attention of Hal Wallis, the legendary movie producer. Wallis is probably best known for producing *Casablanca* and winning an Academy Award for it, but that is just one in a very extensive line of significant movies he produced. He was nominated a whopping sixteen times for Oscars and seven times for Golden Globes. He won two Golden Globes for Best Picture and was honored with the Cecil B. DeMille Award for lifetime achievement in 1975.

I was dying to find out how the two met.

"I was playing a small club, and at that point I didn't have an agent or manager or anybody," Polly said. "Clarence Freed came in, heard me sing, and said he'd like to handle my career. I said, 'Great. Fine.' And Clarence sent a picture of me and a recording to all the well-known producers in Hollywood. I had just recorded a wild hillbilly song: 'Honky Tonking.' The picture was a very glamorous shot of me in a low-cut dress with my hair swept to one side and long rhinestone earrings. So here was this very sophisticated-looking girl and this honky tonk song.

"One of the producers he sent it to was Hal Wallis, and he was kind of mesmerized. He asked me to come in. I met him, and he signed me that same day. He put me in my first three movies—with Martin and Lewis." Those films were *At War with the Army, That's My Boy,* and *The Stooge.*

"I adored Dean Martin more than life itself, and I always played his wife or girlfriend, but I had a very hard time with Jerry." What was the friction there? I asked. "Jerry really wanted to screw anybody he worked with, and that was just the way it was. Jerry made my life a living hell, because I wouldn't play ball with him. Every day on the set was so horrendous that I finally walked away. He would just not take 'no' for an answer!"

Polly did a few movies, including *Escape from Fort Bravo* and *Cry of the Haunted,* and then focused on her singing, taking her act to Vegas and the Persian Room in New York.

"At the Persian Room I did a Helen Morgan medley in my act." Helen Morgan had been a troubled but talented torch singer, known for draping herself over the top of a piano and crooning her blues straight from the heart. She died at the age of forty-one.

"That was really something. I was under contract to MGM, and they were going to do *The Helen Morgan Story*. When I heard that, I went to meet with Mervyn LeRoy, who was a big time producer at MGM, and I tried to convince him I should play it. He explained that I was way too young to play that part—and I was—but I also didn't have enough experience. It got me started putting this medley together because, when

Polly Bergen was a smash hit wherever she performed, from the "big rooms" in Las Vegas to the Persian Room in NYC.

I looked into her story, I found out she was this incredible torch singer, and that was the music I loved to sing. I became fascinated with her and immediately put her music into my act. As a matter of fact I closed my act with it. It was a tremendous asset in the show.

"So, I had just finished my act in the Persian Room, and all of a sudden I get a call from downstairs that there a little old woman who'd like to come up and see me. I said, 'Who is she?' And they said, 'She's Helen Morgan's mother.' I said, 'Oh, my God.'

"She came up, and she was this little old lady. She sat down and explained how moved she had been by the medley I had done. We started talking about Helen, and during the conversation I told her how badly I had wanted to play the part, but Warner Brothers had already bought the film rights, and they were going to do the film. 'Well you know,' she said, 'no one's bought the television rights.' I said, 'No kidding?'

"So right then and there I bought the television rights. I paid twice what they paid for the movie rights—they stole those. I immediately sat down and started getting as much information from her as I could. Then I hired a writer to write the script.

"Now, all of this was on my own. I hadn't sold it to anyone. I was paying for it and hiring writers and all that. Then I went out and tried to sell it, and no one would buy it because they didn't think it was interesting, and they didn't think my name was big enough to carry a television show like that on my own."

"They were probably right, but I kept trying and trying, and finally I decided I'd just sell it, and they wouldn't have to cast me in it. Just so I could get some of my money back. I had well over a million dollars invested in it. About that time *Playhouse 90* was being produced by a friend of mine, Martin Manulis, and I called him and talked to him about it. He said, 'Let me see who I can get interested.' And he piqued the interest of George Roy Hill, who went on become a very famous director. They then sold it to *Playhouse 90* on CBS and went looking for someone to play Helen. There wasn't anyone around who both acted and sang. There just weren't any acting singers. So I lucked into playing it. That's how it ended up on the air. That was the mid-1950s.

"I played the Persian Room a few times more; the last time was in 1965, with Sandler and Young, and that was the last time I ever sang on stage. I retired from singing after my last show at the Persian Room and concentrated on acting. In *Morgan*, I played a very dramatic role, and it was that show that made me a name. [And it won her an Emmy Award.] It was then that I became known as a dramatic actor."

"One of my fondest memories of the Persian Room was the night that David O. Selznick was in the audience. After the show I received a handwritten note from him that said, 'Tonight a star is born.' He never hired me for one of his films, but that note was inspirational."

Not one to retire and take up knitting, Polly continued working in her later years. She had recurring roles on *Desperate Housewives*—which she said was "great fun"— and *The Sopranos*. In 2001, she starred in the Broadway revival of *Follies*. One of her final performances was at a charity event. "Phyllis Newman put it together," she told me. "I was a little nervous, but once I started singing 'The Party's Over,' a theme song of mine, I felt like I did at twenty. My voice was pretty good."

· · · ·

DIAHANN CARROLL, WHO left us in 2019, also turned one of her performances at the Persian Room into a record: *The Persian Room Presents Diahann Carroll.* The recording was supervised by Don Costa, the act staged by Phil Moore, and Peter Matz led the orchestra.

At age ten, Diahann, born Carol Diann Johnson in the Bronx, received a scholarship from the Metropolitan Opera and started learning the fundamentals of singing and performing at the High School of Music and Art. During that same time, she modeled for various Johnson Publication magazines including *Ebony* and *Jet.* After high school she enroll at New York University with the intent of studing sociology, but the allure of entertaining couldn't compete with sitting in a classroom.

After winning the TV talent competition *Chance of a Lifetime* three weeks in a row, she left with $3,000 and a singing engagement at the Latin Quarter. She was just seventeen years old.

Diahann's Broadway debut was in Truman Capote's 1954 *House of Flowers.* In 1962 she earned a Tony Award for her performance in the Richard Rodgers musical *No Strings.*

— 93 —

In these ads for Diahann Carroll's shows of the late '50s and early '60s, you can see the evolution of her look from sweet to sophisticated.

She made her film debut in *Carmen Jones*, and in 1968 she was the first African- American actress to star in her own television series, *Julia*, for which she won a Golden Globe.

When we met, Diahann and I chitchatted about the weather, and the transition from East Coast to West. Then we got down to business.

"I remember having my very first meeting about the possibility of my appearance at the Persian Room. I think maybe there had been one other Afro-American female prior to my arrival. From the tinkling glasses and the china and beautiful room, it was exciting on so many levels. It was a thrill to stand offstage and hear the orchestra strike up the band, knowing it was time to go on and do my show.

"In 1959 I didn't have a choreographer. In those days, it was stand in front of the microphone and sing. Later came choreographers."

Jule Styne, the famed songwriter and lyricist, attended Diahann's opening night at the Persian Room and was clearly impressed. "This beautiful, fragile, delicately feminine young women singing 'Heat Wave' made us believe in her, as the most dangerous *femme terrible* became a lyrical, wistful maiden in love singing 'Misty,' and a charming child-woman singing 'Goody, Goody.' It was a *total* performance. She became all these personalities, and we in the audience believed in her."

Diahann's first song of the night was "Everything's Coming Up Roses," which just so happens to be a very popular Jule Styne song.

"I can't help but notice," I mentioned, "the difference in the ads the Persian Room put out in 1959 and then in 1961 and 1963. In the 1959 ad, you looked very sweet and all wide-eyed, but then *very* sophisticated a few years later."

"In 1959 I was at a very young place. Good God—1959! I was working all the time and felt very fortunate to have that in my life. I was married—fairly recently married. It was a wonderful time for me personally because I was married to Monte Kay, a very caring person who was invested in the work I was learning to do.

"I had a baby in 1960 and was a working mother. My husband and I were trying to have a family life. I had no idea what I had gotten into there. I thought it was easily done."

"You were ahead of your time," I noted. During the '60s, women were just starting to think we could do it all.

"I don't know how any of us did it. I entertained in the suite—we had nightly cocktail parties—and the hotel was wonderful about that because we had some unbelievable people who came to see the show. The Kennedys came, Judy Garland, Josephine Baker came a few times—just everyone. It was just a glass of champagne after the show with friends who came to say hello.

"I worked at the Persian Room on and off for nine years, and it was always a very exciting time for everyone. The move into the Plaza included my family, toys, nanny, and assistants as well as music, all there for the big move!

"One thing I remember very clearly is that after my daughter reached a certain age we learned to use the Plaza hallways as a park, because very often it was snowing or storming out. Suzanne and I played baseball in 'our' park—the hall. We would take the baseball bat and softball and play. It was safe because there weren't any windows to break. The hotel hallways were very large, so we had a good practice area.

"My daughter was named by the entire staff the 'Black Eloise of the Plaza.' It was wonderful because she could move all over the hotel. There was a period when even her cat lived there. Everyone made her feel so at home. It was her home, and she thought it was her house! She was too young for pranks, but she did skip all over the lobby."

In wrapping up our conversation, Diahann shared that at one time she thought the Plaza the perfect spot to commit suicide.

What?!

"It was really adorable because I took one sleeping pill and a bottle of Cristal Champagne and went to the Plaza to kill myself. I think I knew I was playing a game. But I wanted a certain gentleman to feel very remorseful about how he had treated me. My friend who went with me—to the Plaza to kill myself—was my neighbor, Mrs. Miles Davis."

"Who was the gentleman who treated you so poorly?" I asked.

"You noticed I left that out! Well, all the Champagne did was make us giggle. We fell asleep, and the next morning we woke up, had a beautiful breakfast, and left the hotel."

In the 1980s Diahann stirred up trouble weekly as Dominique Deveraux on *Dynasty* and later its spin-off, *The Colbys*. Speaking strictly for myself, I tuned in weekly, not knowing if I'd love or hate Dominique's shenanigans

The beautiful and talented Diahann Carroll called the Plaza her second home as she matured from ingenue on Broadway to headliner at the Persian Room to groundbreaking star on television.

but always knowing I'd covet the wonderful Nolan Miller costumes she'd be wearing.

Diahann is famous for looking fabulous, and even fashion critic Richard Blackwell, who was sparing (to say the least) in his praise, called her "possibly the most perfect woman" and included her on his best-dressed list often.

On April 21, 2010, Diahann gave a live concert to benefit the Annenberg Theater at the Palm Springs Art Museum. The one-woman show has been shown numerous times on PBS as part of its fund-raising programs. Fans could also catch Diahann in a recurring role on the USA Network series *White Collar* from 2008 to '14. Like so many of the stars I talked to for this book, it is difficult to believe Diahann is no longer with us. Her influence as an artist, fashion icon, and groundbreaker certainly remains.

.   .   .   .

BY 1957, THIRTY-NINE million American households had a television, and most of them were tuned to *American Bandstand*, hosted by Dick Clark. He was delivering recording stars right into our living rooms and we loved it. The first song he played nationally was Jerry Lee Lewis's "Whole Lotta Shaking Going On," and his first guests were Billy Williams and the Chordettes.

The Academy Awards were televised for the first time in 1953, when Audrey Hepburn got the Best Actress award for *Roman Holiday*, and Best Picture went to *From Here to*

Eternity. The Grammys were inaugurated in 1958, with Best Male Performance honors going to Perry Come for "Catch a Falling Star." Ella Fitzgerald owned Best Female for *Ella Fitzgerald Sings the Irving Berlin Songbook.*

The end result of all the media exposure was the drive to see our favorite stars in person, in nightclubs, and supper clubs. And that was very good news for the Persian Room.

Some other Persian Room performers from the 1950s:

Edith Adams
Count Basie
Gilbert Becaud
George Burns and
 Gracie Allen
Mindy Carson
Carol Channing
Wally Cox
Pierre and Anna
 D'Angelo
Jane Froman
Genevieve
Bob Hope
Burl Ives
Evelyn Knight
Beatrice Kraft and
 Her Dancers
Elsa Lanchester
Dick LaSalle and
 Orchestra
Lilo
Denise Lor
Kyle MacDonald
George Maharis
Jana Mason
Mata and Hari
Mary McCarty
Marie McDonald
Sal Mineo
Mark Monte and
 His Continentals

Jane Morgan
Katyna Raniere
Johnnie Ray
Mary Raye and
　Naldi
Reyes and Los
　Chavales

Lillian Roth
Jean Sablon
Dorothy Shay
Herb Shriner
Yvette

CHAPTER FOUR

Jazz at the Plaza

The incomparable Billie Holiday, best known to the world as "Lady Day," at her final recording session, shortly after the legendary "Jazz at the Plaza" concert.

The story of American music is, by and large, a set of flukes and accidents, some of which take on genuine significance in retrospect. When Benny Goodman played Carnegie Hall in 1938, no one knew it would open that storied venue's doors to many genres of new music—not only jazz, but also pop, folk, and even rock-and-roll. When George Wein produced the first Newport Jazz Festival in 1954, it was anybody's guess if he could make it through a single season; no one would have predicted that the annual event would remain a vital part of the music scene for some seventy years—even beyond the long lifespan of the impresario.

Jazz at the Plaza also started as a novelty, but unlike Jazz at Carnegie Hall or Newport, that's all it was destined to be. The one-nighter—an amazing three-hour concert held on September 9, 1958, that virtually nobody was aware of—would never be repeated. It might even have been forgotten, if not for a recording issued fifteen years after the fact. But it can't be denied: this once-in-a-lifetime gathering of major stars who had never worked together or even appeared on the same bill remains one of the most special nights in the history of jazz. It isn't an exaggeration to call it legendary.

So, who played? A very lucky invited audience was treated to more than a half dozen of the biggest names in jazz history; Miles Davis, Duke Ellington, Billie Holiday, John Coltrane, Cannonball Adderley, Bill Evans, and Jimmy Rushing, not to mention Johnny Hodges, Paul Gonsalves, Clark Terry, and the entire Ellington Orchestra. All in one room on one night. Thankfully recorded in state-of-the-art stereo.

In the preceding twelve months, two other watershed events threw a spotlight on the jazz community that brought the art form to a wider audience. The first was the December 1957 episode of CBS's *Lively Arts* called "The Sound of Jazz." The second was the August 1958 photo session for *Esquire* Magazine titled "A Great Day in Harlem"—a festive gathering of virtually every notable jazz artist then alive, with the notable exceptions of Duke Ellington and Miles Davis.

As if to make up for their absence in the picture, the two legendary bandleaders were the primary focus of the Jazz at the Plaza event. Irving Townsend, its primary organizer, reminisced about it in 1973, describing it as an informal get-together hosted by Columbia records to pay tribute to its artists. Attendance was by invitation only. "It was a time when jazz in America had never been more popular, and at a place in which jazz had never been at all," Townsend recalled. He and his colleague, Teo Macero, selected the Persian Room for exactly that reason. Even more than The Copa or The Latin Quarter, The Persian Room featured the toniest and most sophisticated headliners; Kay Thompson and the Williams Brothers, Celeste Holm, Polly Bergen—prior to that September evening, the jazziest artist to appear there was probably Eartha Kitt. It was the kind of club that catered to many an expense account, especially from Madison Avenue advertising agencies and midtown media moguls. Executives from the big name firms—NBC, RCA, BBD&O, and CBS—all took business guests out to many a multiple martini meal in that age of *Mad Men* and *The Apartment*. It must be noted, also, that the location was particularly convenient for staffers at Columbia, which was then located at the corner of Seventh Avenue and 52nd Street.

. . . .

THE FORCE BEHIND the jazz department at Columbia Records was a bald-headed Armenian immigrant, Yale graduate, and World War II veteran named George Avakian. For a dozen years after the end of the war, he steadily built up the jazz division at Columbia to the point where it was well-respected artistically, and a powerful force commercially. After the rise in popularity of the 12" LP format in the mid-1950s, Avakian marshaled an amazing roster of major names and produced albums now considered classics, by such legends as Duke Ellington, Miles Davis, Erroll Garner, Louis Armstrong, Dave Brubeck, and Jimmy Rushing. Despite his success, by 1958 Avakian felt underappreciated by the label's upper management. He ended up leaving early that year, and over the next six decades would go on to produce for a number of other major labels until his death at 98 in 2017.

As if to answer any question as to the status of Columbia's jazz department after Avakian's departure, the label set out to offer a triumphant answer in live musical form. After all, it still boasted the greatest roster of jazz legends—why not show them off? The planning fell to the division's two main producers: Irving Townsend, who had been Avakian's protegee, and Teo Macero, a composer and saxophonist who would later earn a place in history for his work with Miles Davis. It was their belief that a concert featuring their top-tier talent, held at a plush, upscale venue like the Persian Room—not that there was anything remotely like the Persian Room—was sure to make headlines.

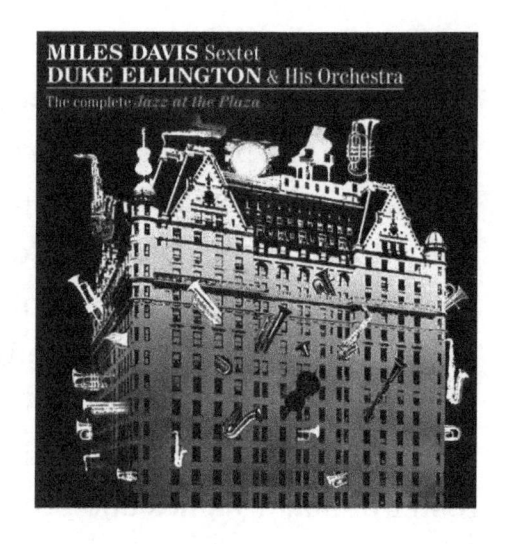

"Jazz at the Plaza" is a tale of two different time periods; first as a time capsule demonstrating where jazz was on that evening in 1958, and secondly, where it was in 1973, when most (but far from all) of the amazing music recorded that night was finally released. Both Ellington and Davis were still active in 1973, though Davis was creating a very different kind of music at that point and Ellington was nearing the end of his run (he would be gone by May 1974.) Releasing the material in 1973 was a nod to an era that was fast receding from memory, and The Persian Room itself would close its doors the following year.

It's clear, too, that Irving Townsend's memory had faded significantly in the fifteen years between the event and the release of the recordings. His liner notes include a number of errors, including the identity of the venue itself: "The place, of course, was the Edwardian Room of the Plaza hotel," he wrote, "a dining room which normally holds a few dozen guests." He also noted that the event took place in July, while in fact it was held on September 9, 1958, but no matter. It's the music that makes it worth remembering.

The four major participants in the event included its two famous bandleaders, Ellington and Davis; and two star vocalists, the great blues "shouter" Jimmy Rushing and the magnificent Billie Holiday, all of whom had two things in common: first, the obvious fact that they were all then under contract to Columbia Records; and secondly, all four had gone through fallow periods in the early to mid-1950s (Rushing had briefly retired after the Count Basie band broke up in 1950) before resuscitating their careers.

The evening was divided into three sets. First, the Duke Ellington Orchestra played about thirty minutes of brilliant original instrumental music. Then, the Miles Davis Sextet took the stage for four extended numbers lasting about forty-five minutes in total. The final set was performed by the Ellington band—including two of its own singers, Ozzie Bailey and Lil Greenwood—along with the two superstar guest vocalists, Rushing and Holiday.

The music started at the unfashionable hour of 5:00 pm, and Duke and his men began with his famous theme song, "Take the A Train." They concluded with the curiously titled "Jones," featuring Clark Terry and what Duke called his "finger-snapping bit," in which he instructed the audience on how and when to snap. The rest of the set consisted of brand-new work that he wouldn't record until a year later.

The first set ended about 5:40 or 5:45, and Miles Davis took the stage at 6:00. This was the classic Davis Sextet— just about the most star-studded jazz ensemble of all time— with the leader on trumpet, joined by alto saxophonist Julian "Cannonball" Adderley, tenor saxophonist John Coltrane, pianist Bill Evans, bassist Paul Chambers, and drummer Jimmy Cobb. This was the group that would record the masterpiece *Kind of Blue* a few months later. Davis was always a man in transition, and at this moment especially so, as evidenced in a set that ping-ponged in style and consisted of four pieces— two jazz standards and two highly personal takes on iconic show tunes: "If I Were a Bell" from *Guys and Dolls*; "Oleo," Sonny Rollins's famous variations on "I Got Rhythm"; Richard Rodgers' "My Funny Valentine"; and Thelonious Monk's "Straight, No Chaser."

Jazz made a brief but memorable appearance at the Persian Room in 1958, when Duke Ellington (second from left), Jimmy Rushing (third from left) and a host of other jazz greats assembled at a party hosted by Columbia Records. Lucky for us, the event yielded two albums—one headlined by the Duke and one by Miles Davis.

The third short set began when Ellington's band and guests took the stage around 7:00. The 1973 LP *Jazz at the Plaza, Vol II* includes roughly twenty-three minutes of music from this set, but discographies indicate that there was at least that much more that has never been released.

The one disappointment of the evening was that the two major ensembles never performed together. It would have been historic to hear Davis soloing in front of the Ellington aggregation, as fellow bandleader Tommy Dorsey once did, or to have Duke sit-in with the Miles group, as he later did with Louis Armstrong's All Stars. Rather than cooperation, their mutual presence seems to have inspired a healthy dose of competition.

This was noticed by many observers, including the novelist, essayist, and critic Ralph Ellison, who was present. "I was at a party given by Columbia Records at the Plaza recently," he wrote in a letter to colleague Albert Murray, "where they presented Duke, Miles Davis, Jimmy Rushing, and Billie Holiday and it was murder."

Ellison, was forty-five at the time, and enjoying the success of his highly acclaimed novel *Invisible Man*. He had grown up on Ellington, Count Basie, and the big bands, and clearly regarded the Duke as the established master on the bill and Miles the cheeky interloper. "Duke signified on Davis all through his numbers," he wrote, "and his trumpeters and saxophonists went after him like a bunch of hustlers in a Georgia skin game fighting with razors. Only Cannonball Adderley sounded as though he might have some of the human qualities which sound unmistakably in the Ellington band. And no question of numbers was involved. They simply had more to say, and a hundred more ways in which to say it."

Townsend hit a similar note when he wrote, "Duke returned to the bandstand after the Davis Sextet's brilliant finale, and if you know how the Ellington mind works, it was not surprising that he came back with trumpets blaring."

If the discographies are correct, Ellington began the third set with another "Take the A-Train," followed by two numbers featuring baritone Ozzie Bailey, who sang with the band from roughly 1956-1959. Bailey provided vocals for "Autumn Leaves," presumably in French and then English; and "What Else Can You Do with a Drum?," from Ellington's 1956 theatrical work, *A Drum Is a Woman*.

Then came two instrumental numbers, each a spectacular feature for one of the band's acclaimed soloists. "El Gato" spotlighted trumpeter Willian "Cat" Anderson, probably Duke's flashiest player, who could play faster and higher than anybody. This evening, "El Gato" was even more sensational than usual, presented as a kind of duel between Anderson and the band's other high-octane trumpeter, the great Clark Terry, and demonstrating what Ellison meant when he noted that Duke's trumpeters cut Miles Davis to ribbons.

"All of Me" showed off a different kind of virtuosity as a spotlight for the band's great blues-and-ballads specialist, the immortal Johnny Hodges. Following the intro, Hodges leapt right in and played with his usual mastery as well as exquisite soulfulness—probably more of it than anybody that whole evening, with the possible exception of Billie Holiday. The whole performance lasted under three minutes—the length of a single—but Hodges communicated more passion and feeling in that time than most performers can accomplish at ten times the length. The piece ended with a conclusive cymbal crash from longtime Ducal drummer Sam Woodyard.

"We now have the extreme pleasure or the responsibility, of accompanying a great artist to whom we are bidding *bon voyage*, Jimmy Rushing," said Ellington at that point, referring to the fact that the great blues singer was about to leave for Europe.

"Jimmy had always wanted to sing with Duke," Townsend recalled, " and this was his chance."

Clearly, the two of them had prepared for the occasion with at least a casual rehearsal. The two tunes they prepared became three on the album. The first was a somewhat obscure blues number from the Ellington bandbook, "Go Away Blues"; the second was one of Rushing's signature pieces, which he sang with virtually every band and in every context, changing the lyrics from night to night. At the Persian Room, he sang a few choruses as "Hello, Little Girl," creating an occasion for great playing from Clark Terry, Paul Gonsalves, and others.

When the crowd refused to stop applauding, Duke told Jimmy, "Sing some blues!" and he continued in the same vein. The encore, which started with the familiar line, "I Love to Hear My Baby Call My Name," was listed as a separate song on the album.

Alas, Billie Holiday didn't perform with the Ellington aggregation, although the two had a long history together. Instead, she brought her regular accompanist, Mal Waldron, as well as trumpeter Buck Clayton, a frequent collaborator. The bassist and drummer seem to have been Chambers and Cobb from the Davis Sextet.

In the last few years of her life Holiday was up and down as a performer, but she was in great form that night, making it a shame that she sang only two numbers. The first one was, "When Your Lover Has Gone,"—which both she and Sinatra learned from Louis Armstrong—and then came her own "Don't Explain." According to Townsend, "She arrived late and didn't stay long, but she was among friends."

Townsend indicated that after Holiday, the Duke played "Take the A-Train" one more time, and the evening came to an abrupt halt—"That was the kind of party it was," according to Townsend. Yet the discography suggests that there was one additional instrumental, "Hi Fi Fo Fum," a feature for drummer Sam Woodyard that the band had most famously played and recorded a few months earlier at Newport. Then came two numbers for Lil Greenwood, a singer who toured with the band for only a few months: "Won't You Come Home Bill Bailey" and "Walkin' and Singin' the Blues." The sequence seems odd, as it would have been highly insensitive for Duke to expect a singer to follow Jimmy Rushing and Billie Holiday, but who knows?

The discography also reveals that the set concluded not with "A-Train" but with another performance of "Jones" and the finger-snapping bit.

And that, apparently, was it. The event went largely unnoticed at the time, except by those lucky enough to be

Billie Holiday and John Coltrane were also on hand for the Persian Room's brief foray into jazz.

there, and was quickly forgotten. There were two notices—in the industry publications *Billboard* and *Downbeat*. The former described the evening as "the first self-liquidating press party in the record industry," and both noted that Columbia was planning to issue excerpts. They weren't entirely wrong, except that it would be two LPs and it would take another fifteen years before they made it into record stores.

. . . .

WE MUST BE grateful to Irv Townsend for three things: for producing the event to begin with—and in the loveliest room possible; for making sure it was recorded in state-of-the-art stereophonic hi-fi sound; and for eventually releasing about eighty-five minutes of the historic occasion.

In Townsend's recollection, the event had been "too small for strangers, too brief for friends. But long enough to say hello before everybody had to be somewhere else." He concluded by offering an enchanting mini-portrait of Ellington relaxing afterwards, enjoying one of his favorite indulgences—other than music and women: "For some of us it ended down the street at Reuben's," he wrote, referring to the famous deli on 59th and Madison, "where we watched as Duke worked his way through a soul bowl piled with assorted scoops of ice cream. 'To lubricate his ears,' he explained, and of course, we believe him."

CHAPTER FIVE

The Plaza on Record

A rare photo of the divine Lisa Kirk performing her fan dance in the middle of the Persian Room floor.

Miles Davis and Duke Ellington weren't the only great artists to record important works at the Persian Room. Perhaps artists and producers felt the venue would lend a bit of panache, validity, or sophistication to the result—or maybe they simply enjoyed its cool vibe. Certainly, the fact that it held just 200 people made it an easier environment to control, acoustically speaking. The excitement of a live and appreciative audience was there, but background sounds were easier to mute than at, say, a stadium, concert hall, or the famed Apollo.

Eartha Kitt in Person at the Plaza was not Kitt's first live album; there was at least one earlier one—*C'est Si Bon, Live in Tivoli*, recorded at the famous concert hall in Copenhagen and released by EMI Columbia in Europe in 1963—but it never made its way to the States. It's the Plaza album, full of Kitt's hits and signature numbers, that everyone remembers, and rightly so. It is a perfect documentation of her nightclub act of the mid-1960s, which many consider to be, as Louis Armstrong would say, the height of her height. It's also a perfect mix of everything that made Kitt great, including international exoticism, seduction, and high comedy.

In Person at the Plaza was conducted by the star's musical director, David Saxon, who also wrote "Champagne Taste" and is shown behind her on the cover, holding a baton and looking somewhat like Milton Berle. It's a well-balanced blend of songs written expressly for Kitt, along with others she acquired indirectly. She starts with "Sell Me," a perfect piece of special material from Bart Howard, whose lyrics touch on familiar themes in Kitt's signature songs, setting her up as a highly self-entitled femme fatale. She spends the whole song explaining in great detail exactly what she expects from one of her potential lovers, never mentioning anything she's going to give him in return.

"I Wanna Be Evil," next in the set, was a Kitt perennial for good reason: it's one of the funniest and most exciting numbers she ever performed—like a very adult song sung by a little girl, or possible the other way around. "Waray, Waray." by contrast, comes off as genuinely innocent— perhaps because it is sung in the Filipino language of Tagalog and sounds like a children's counting song. "How Could You Believe Me?" by Alan Jay Lerner and Burton Lane is the comic highlight from the 1951 Fred Astaire movie *Royal Wedding*.

Other cuts captured live that night include such classic Kitt crowd pleasers as "Come on-a My House," "Old-Fashioned Girl" and "C'est Si Bon"—her biggest hit ever, and one of her only two top-ten singles, along with "Santa Baby." A delightful surprise is the klezmer classic "Rumania, Rumania" sung in Yiddish. In the true spirit of the genre, Kitt squeezed the notes in and out of all kinds of kinky pentatonic places, moving Persian Room patrons to a veritable frenzy.

Eartha Kitt in Person at the Plaza captures the great entertainer at a particularly strong moment: at the height of her vocal powers and before her musical gifts would be eclipsed by her fame as the first and greatest actress to play Batman's nemesis, Catwoman (she would also achieve a kind of infamy as the most prominent African American star to be, essentially, blackballed by a Democratic presidential administration—that of Lyndon Johnson—as a result of her outspokenness at a White House event).

Having seen her live several times at the Café Carlyle and at her 80th Birthday extravaganza at Carnegie Hall in 2007, we can attest that she was herself—both ravishingly sexy and completely innocent right up until the end.

· · · ·

LISA KIRK (1923-1990) was a vivacious entertainer who made her name on Broadway just in time to benefit from the golden age of posh supper clubs and TV variety shows. It was an era that didn't last very long, but career-wise, as in everything else, Kirk's timing was perfect.

So too was her sense of balance; she was most famous for roles in two important shows: the long-suffering nurse in Rodgers and Hammerstein's 1947 musical, *Allegro* (not a big moneymaker but a theatrical milestone nevertheless) and Cole Porter's blockbuster *Kiss Me, Kate* a year later. She also appeared in two noteworthy flops, Meredith Wilson's *Here's Love* (1963) and Jerry Herman's *Mack and Mabel* (1974), and could be spotted on television throughout the 1950s and 60s, from *The Ed Sullivan Show* to a guest starring spot on *Bewitched*.

She was one of only a handful of female singers who put out an album recorded live at the Plaza—an indication that one had reached the top of the show-biz food chain.

Released by MGM Records in 1959, *Lisa Kirk Sings at the Plaza* is a wonderful album but a curious one. There is applause at the end of each of the ten songs, and an occasional ripple of laughter after a funny line in a lyric—but the crowd noises sound very artificial, almost like a laugh track in a period sitcom. As heretical as it sounds, we're willing to bet that the ten tracks were recorded in a studio and not in the Persian Room at all.

By 1959, Kirk was widely known as a mainstay on Broadway and television, though not film or recordings. For whatever reason, she would never get a shot at a juicy movie role (nor would her *Kiss Me Kate* co-stars, Alfred Drake and Patricia Morison), and although she had made a handful of singles for RCA, she had not yet done an album of her own. She did, however, enjoy eight full runs at the Persian Room.

Her career hit its peak in 1959-60, with appearances on several high-profile variety shows—and that's when MGM decided to give her a crack at a full-length album. Rather than tout her as the star of *Kate*, they settled on a "branded" album—the Plaza being the brand in question. And, though *Lisa Kirk Sings at the Plaza* was apparently created in the studio, it should be regarded as an authentic record of her nightclub act, and is a delight from start to finish.

Kirk begins with a real zinger of a special-material number, "I Travel Light," credited to her husband, Bob Wells, and David Saxon. Not only is it an exciting curtain-raiser, the number deftly establishes the character she'll inhabit for the rest of the evening—a privileged but loveable rich girl, somewhat ditzy but self-determined.

Kirk then segues into "I'm Sitting on Top of the World,"

which reinforces the image of the woman who has everything, including talent and beauty. Two classic Cole Porter songs follow, both retooled by Wells with special material. "You'd Be So Nice to Come Home to" is intoned in Kirk's lowest, sexiest voice. There's a brief *parlando* interjection at the end—"I bring you your slippers, I serve you your kippers"—wherein she sounds like "Kate the cursed" in the last speech of *The Taming of the Shrew*.

Porter's "Anything Goes" features a whole new verse:

> Things that once would raise an eyebrow
> Nowadays, wouldn't phase your brow or my brow.
> Today, if Lady Godiva, Lady Godiva should come
>   along,
> Men would say 'she's out of style, her hair's a mile
>   too long.'
> Golden days, olden days, are gone, gone, gone.

Right after the canned-sounding applause, Kirk sings "Hi Lili, Hi-Lo" from the classic 1953 film *Lili* as a very sad and slow waltz. The last offering on Side A is "How Come You Do Me (Like You Do)," co-credited to pioneering jazz-age crooner Gene Austin and his vaudeville partner Roy Bergere. It's an old-time vaudeville-type tune that allows Kirk to wrench up both the volume and the humor, if not the tempo.

Side B commences with one of Kirk's big numbers from *Kiss Me, Kate*, "Why Can't You Behave?" now sung with even more sexual energy than in the show, and again with some special material interpolated. *Kudos* to both Kirk and Wells for having the *chutzpah* to rewrite Cole Porter.

"Good Little Girls" is a great example of the kind of character song that nearly every diva who headlined at the Persian Room sang. It's replete with the humorous contrast of innocence and seductiveness that was a particular hallmark of Eartha Kitt's repertoire, but it could easily have been sung by Kay Thompson, Celeste Holm, or Lainie Kazan. In fact, it was originally for Bette Davis to sing in her one major Broadway show, the 1952 revue *Two's Company*, with music by Vernon Duke, lyrics by Sammy Cahn - and yet more special material by Wells and Saxon. (Spoiler alert: the main thrust of the text is along the lines of, "Good little girls go to Heaven, but smart little girls go to Bergdorf, to Bonwit...") Lines like "I always draw a crowd with / What I've been endowed with" seem to be very specifically describing Ms. Kirk.

Much of the rest of the album is devoted to travel and exotica, and the last number is a spectacular one involving a singing and dancing chorus. "Limehouse Blues" was originally associated with the legendary Gertrude Lawrence and went on to enjoy a dual heritage as an instrumental jazz standard and a dramatic showstopper for such icons as Fred Astaire (*Ziegfeld Follies*) and Julie Andrews (playing Lawrence in *Star!*). At the time it was written, it was considered to be sympathetic to the people it describes—the Asian underclass in the West—but it is difficult not to hear it as insensitive and patronizing today. Kirk's performance of it is solidly in the theatrical tradition, but has plenty of rhythm, nonetheless. It omits a particularly

Eartha Kitt purred and growled her way to legendary status, thanks in no small part to her engagements at the Persian Room.

offensive verse in favor of some new material by Wells and Saxon—still quite "faux-Asian" in effect.

Hollywood missed a good bet when it passed over Lisa Kirk. Like Ann Miller, who assumed her role in the movie version of *Kiss Me, Kate*, she was a terrific dancer, but more than that, a first-class singer with a throaty, sexy sound. Alas, her sole prominent movie performance was off-screen, supplying the singing voice of Rosalind Russell—who was almost twenty years her senior—in Warner Bros.' misguided, big-budget rendering of the Broadway hit *Gypsy* (1962).

She came back to Broadway in two unsuccessful shows, first replacing Janis Paige in the musical version of *Miracle on 34th Street* titled *Here's Love* (1963-'64), and then in a supporting role in Jerry Herman's cult show, *Mack and Mabel* (1974). But there's no doubt that she was at the peak of both her powers and her acclaim when she was a beloved regular at the Persian Room.

. . . .

DIAHANN CARROLL WAS only twenty-four when she appeared at the Persian Room in 1960 and her reminiscences are included elsewhere in this book. *The Persian Room presents Diahann Carroll* was her fourth "solo" album, and unlike Lisa Kirk's, the fine print states clearly, "Recorded live at the Persian Room, Plaza Hotel, New York, February 4, 1960."

Jule Styne—whose hit show *Gypsy* was then still running on Broadway, and who's next Broadway success, *Do-Re-Mi*, would open later in the year—was there on opening night. It's quite possible that he'd been tipped off that Carroll was opening with "Everything's Coming Up Roses" from *Gypsy*, but, whatever the reason for his presence, the legendary songwriter was so impressed that he offered to write the liner notes for the resultant album. Anyone who knew Styne understood what a big deal this was. Although he could effortlessly spin out amazing melodies, he struggled with the written word and rarely committed to such an effort.

The first half of Carroll's album is suffused with the coy, sex-kitten attitude you'd expect from a young female headliner at the Persian Room—though she comes off as somewhat more innocent than either Lisa Kirk, who preceded her, or Eartha Kitt, who followed. After "Roses," she tells the crowd, "Just about here every night, we change, and we sing something kind of romantic and just a little bit mushy, 'cause we like mushy songs!" Her pronunciation of the key word as "mooshy" makes it sound very sweet and seductive indeed, yet the only song we'd really characterize that way is "Misty," the Erroll Garner instrumental transformed via lyrics by Johnny Burke into a pop hit and jazz standard.

There follows a comic song by Harold Rome called "Shopping Around" (from the show *Wish You Were Here*) and an arch song of romantic revenge, Johnny Mercer's "Goody Goody." A long monologue about an innocent girl who meets the scoundrel of her dreams seamlessly leads into Rodgers and Hart's "I Wish I Were in Love Again." She begins that one in a whisper and ends it with an effectively belted climax.

Side Two begins with "All or Nothing at All," the jazziest number on the disc. Singing in a clipped, up-tempo style that builds to a wild and swinging climax, Carroll intertwines elements of jazz and black show business in manner reminiscent of Sammy Davis, Jr., who must have been an influence on her.

And speaking of the legacy of black showbiz, the rest of the album, surprisingly, is all songs from the book of the great Ethel Waters. There's no mention of this in the album's notes or the singer's spoken patter, but it was clearly no coincidence. Our suspicion is that Carroll planned the lineup as a tribute to Ms. Waters, but that the living legend—who was never known to be charitable to younger singers—demurred from the attention.

The Waters material is separated into five tracks, two of which are medleys. The first medley includes "Am I Blue," introduced by Waters in the 1929 musical *On With the Show* (1929); the up-tempo "Taking a Chance on Love"; and the ballad "Happiness Is a Thing Called Joe." The second medley begins with "Dinah," introduced by Waters at the Plantation Club in 1925, followed by "After You've Gone" from the *Cotton Club Parade of 1933*, and Harold Arlen's "Stormy Weather."

"Heat Wave," written for Waters for the 1933 Broadway revue *As Thousands Cheer*, was an unusually elaborate song for its composer, Irving Berlin, consisting of a verse, a chorus, and extended semi-spoken patter section. Carroll begins with the patter and, after a sequence of semi-erotic moans, chants, "It's so hot the weatherman will tell us a record's been made. ..." Then she launches into the well-known chorus ("We're having a heat wave..."). It adds up to an exciting performance set to a very contemporary-sounding mambo beat that's more Havana than Martinique.

These are the last words we hear Ms. Carroll sing before the orchestra swells into an instrumental reprise of "Happiness Is a Thing Called Joe" to play her graciously off the stage.

Carroll was just starting out when she recorded this wonderful album. Still to come were many more performances on film and television as well as more albums—including *A Tribute to Ethel Waters*. Tellingly, it was released in 1978, a few months after Waters' death, when the diva was in no position to interfere.

. . . .

Lisa Kirk, Eartha Kitt, and Diahann Carroll were all-around entertainers—triple threats as singer/dancer/actresses with long and varied resumes. By contrast, Vikki

Diahann Carroll poses with recording mogul Clive Davis.

Carr was (and is) primarily a pop vocalist and hit-maker. She didn't dance, tell jokes or play roles other than herself, but focused on crafting hit singles and highly bestselling full-length albums (ten of the former and thirteen of the latter). What's more, as her performances on *The Ed Sullivan Show, The Hollywood Palace*, and a number of other variety shows make clear, she was a terrific live performer as well. (Sullivan was in the house when she made the live recording we're about to discuss.)

Carr's parents were Mexican, a fact that she jokes about on *For Once in My Life—Live at the Persian Room*. The and, in the tradition of that country, her full name at birth (in El Paso, 1940) was a very long one: Florencia Vicenta de Casillas-Martínez Cardona. In fact, she makes a joke of it on this album. (And that name, remember, doesn't include any of her three husbands.) This album contains several songs from the Iberian diaspora: "Yesterday I Heard the Rain," the work of Armando Manzanero, "the Irving Berlin of Mexico"; and "Manhã de Carnaval," by the celebrated Brazilian guitarist Luiz Bonfá, first heard as the theme for the classic 1959 film *Orfeu Negro (Black Orpheus)*. As Ms. Carr says, there have been "so many versions" of this song. In fact, it was one of the hits that helped establish the Bossa Nova as an international phenomenon. Her personal favorite, she notes, was by Jack Jones, another Persian Room veteran still very much with us. Although she admits regret that she can't sing the song in the original Portuguese, she renders it beautifully in Spanish.

Carr's international bent was one of her key assets, along with her lovely and unique voice and flawless intonation and timing. Being bilingual made her more in step with this truly international era of pop music, in which not only British and Brazilian but French, Greek, Italian, Spanish, Mexican, and even Japanese songs were all over the charts. Carr's biggest hit was, in fact, a French song, "It Must Be Him," by the Toulon-born composer Gilbert Bécaud with English lyrics by the New York-born songwriter Mack David.

Ms. Carr's single was a huge hit in 1969, but this live version from the Persian Room is even better, deeper, dramatic and more lived-in, truly a torch song for the ages. (I touch on the back story of how this chart topper came to be included in the mega-hit *"Moonstruck"* in a later chapter.) After the Brazilian song, Carr introduces the celebrities in the house, namely Henny Youngman, Jerry Vale, Ed Sullivan, and Senator Jacob Javits. "Boy!" she quips at the senator, "you really had to know somebody to get that lousy seat!"

The album also includes two British songs. The first is "After Today," with words and music written by Leslie Bricusse for his longtime professional partner Anthony Newley to sing in the 1967 movie musical epic (and epic flop) *Doctor Dolittle.* Carr enlivens it with several exciting key changes. "The Other Man's Grass Is Always Greener," which Carr also performed on *The Hollywood Palace,* is a philosophical ode from the British team of Jackie Trent and Tony Hatch, who were responsible for most of Petula Clark's blockbuster hits of the late 1960s, most famously "I Know a Place" and "Downtown."

Carr delivers completely credible renditions of three of the biggest hits of the era: The Turtles's "Happy Together," the Four Seasons' "Can't Take My Eyes Off of You," and "This Girl's In Love With You." written by Burt Bacharach and Hal David (younger brother of "It Must Be Him" lyricist Mack David) and widely popularized by Herb Alpert. There's also a country-and-western song, Bobby Goldsboro's "With Pen In Hand" which, as she describes in her introduction, represents the genre in that "it tells it like it is." That it does, especially in her impassioned performance here. "Days" was by Anthony Paul Byrne, also known as Paul Byrne, a songwriter and singer who worked in both the country and pop genres in the late 1960s and early '70s.

At least once in each of the Persian Room albums we've discussed, the headlining diva pulls out an old-time vaudeville-type tune—and Carr is no exception. In her case, it's a two-for-one—a medley of "Some of These Days" and "After You've Gone." Both of these songs were written in the 1910s by black songwriters, Henry Creamer and Turner Layton in the first case and Shelton Brooks in the second. Both became jazz standards as well as rabble-rousing diva perennials, and Carr uses them to ratchet up the excitement.

The two songs are thoughtfully intertwined, and when she starts to belt, it's never gratuitous and always genuinely enthralling.

Carr ends as she began, with a larger-than-life rendition of "For Once in My Life"—a number sung by absolutely everyone (or so it seemed) in the late sixties. It's a resounding finish, not only to the record, but to the cycle of four albums emanating from the Persian Room (well . . . Lisa Kirk's gets an asterisk). Just a few years later the era would come to an end, but you'd never know it listening to these four remarkable ladies.

CHAPTER SIX

The 1960s

When the lights go out all over Broadway, The Plaza glows a little brighter.

The Plaza is New York's blazing late show, a Roman candle at midnight, a sentinel against the dawn.

Conversation crackles in the Palm Court after 8. Wit flashes through the red-velvet underground of Plaza 9-. A late supper warms the Oak Room. The volcano mutters in Trader Vic's. And stars come out in the Persian Room.

Torches have been kindled at The Plaza, hearts set afire, bridges burned. It gives a lovely light.

THE PLAZA

An ad for the Plaza from the 1960s.

With some seventy million baby boomers reaching adolescence, the decade of the '60s was nothing if not the age of youth. The conservatism of the 1950s gave way, and anything offbeat, radical, and fresh was embraced by a generation eager to shatter the mold set by their parents. It was one of the most tumultuous decades ever, the young rejecting their parents' values and embracing an optimistic, counter-cultural vision of change. It was a time of political transformation, artistic invention, and social experimentation on a scale never before seen in American history. Women's liberation (abetted by the availability of the Pill), grassroots political action, widespread drug experimentation, and communal living were the more substantial movements afoot. On the style side came bell-bottom jeans and suede jackets, impossibly skimpy miniskirts, long hair for everyone, white leather go-go boots, and a general shift away from the buttoned-down "uniform" of the '50s in favor of a more casual, anything-goes image.

The "Camelot" Kennedy Presidency and the momentum of the civil rights movement made Americans start to feel that anything was possible, until a tragic succession of assassinations as well as the fallout from a nasty faraway war brought us all back to earth.

You might assume that the timeless little boîte known as the Persian Room was immune to the effects of those social tidal waves, but make no mistake, things changed there, too. Well . . . a little bit. Suits replaced tuxedos on stage and in the audience, and short dresses triumphed permanently over evening gowns. As more people commuted in from the suburbs to work, there was often no opportunity to go home and change for a night on the town; business attire became evening wear and has remained so ever since. (More's the pity!)

New York City was the center of the cultural universe the day four shaggy-haired young men stepped off a plane from England and revolutionized music forever. On February 7, 1964, the Beatles checked into the Plaza and stayed for five chaotic days, dodging the paparazzi and frenzied fans as they prepared for their inaugural U.S. appearance on *The Ed Sullivan Show*. After that, the sky was the limit for them—and for rock-and-roll.

Back on earth, Persian Room audiences were exposed to a wider variety of stars and top-notch entertainment than anyone imagined possible. Broadway superstars, pop singers, uproariously funny comedians, mystifying magicians—all had their moment on the jewel box stage.

· · · ·

FLORENCIA BISENTA DE Casillas Martinez Cardona, or as we know her—Vikki Carr—has had over sixty best-selling recordings, earned a Latin Grammy Lifetime Achievement Award, and won three Grammy Awards. Vikki toured with Danny Kaye entertaining the American troops during the Vietnam war, and performed by Royal Command at London's Royal Albert Hall for Queen Elizabeth II. Mind you, that's just a tiny peek at her accomplishments and accolades.

With all her tributes and awards, one that Vikki most appreciates is having her chart-topping hit "It Must Be Him" featured in the movie *Moonstruck*. Who can forget Olympia Dukakis, as the matriarch Rose, muttering, "'Now he's going to play that damn Vikki Carr record, and when he comes to bed he won't touch me.'" I asked Vikki how the song found its way into the iconic film.

"This isn't going to be a short answer," she replied. "At the peak of my success, we were going to do a television special and I was very impressed with Norman Jewison's work. So I wrote and told him that this was my very first fan letter. I let him know how much I loved his work and asked if he would do me the honor of directing the music special for me. I didn't think I'd ever hear back from him, but I received an answer by mail shortly afterward, saying, 'Dear Ms. Carr, this is the first fan letter *I've* ever written, and I'm honored that you'd want me to direct your special.' Unfortunately, he went on to explain that he was in Europe scouting locations for *Fiddler on the Roof*. And that was that. Much later, *Moonstruck* came out and some of my fan club told me I had to see it. Well, I went with a bunch of them, but I had no idea what I was in store for. When 'It Must Be Him' came on, they all stood and clapped. I was so embarrassed but in a delighted and amazed way. So . . . I wrote another letter. 'Dear Mr. Jewison,' I said, 'this is the second fan letter I've ever written, and it's to the same star. Thank you for including me in your movie. I was very moved.' He answered back, and we started a nice repartée. I kidded him for a long time that my song won them their Academy Award!"

On November 13, 1968, Vikki was booked at the Persian Room—not just to sing but to record a live album. "I was more involved than I typically am in doing a great job at the Plaza," she told me, "because of the record. And, wouldn't you know it, the Hong Kong flu was going around and I got the bug. If you listen to *For Once in My Life*, you can vaguely tell I was having throat problems on one or two songs, but only if you know about it. My audience was amazing, and I think they helped me forget and overcome the illness.

"New York can be a tough town, and the Persian Room's bar for excellence was exceptionally high, but this night was fabulous. Everyone came out to see my show: Ed Sullivan, Jerry Vale, Henny Youngman, Bobby Bare, and Senator Jacob Javits, to name a few. I couldn't have felt more supported.

"One of my favorite numbers was from *Carnival*. I told the audience, 'I would now like to sing this for you in the original Portuguese.' There was a dramatic pause and I continued, 'Unfortunately, I can't. So, I'm going to sing it for you in Spanish.' That got a good laugh. For the longest time, I was told, 'Don't talk, just sing.' Well, I asserted myself that night at the Persian Room, and it felt wonderful to claim my voice and create a rapport with my audience. I was fortunate that the Plaza orchestra was top-notch and we augmented it with some of my own guys so the music was outstanding."

One of the songs from *For Once in My Life*, "With Pen in Hand," was issued as a single in February 1969. It was on *Billboard*'s Hot 100 for thirteen weeks, reached number six on its Easy-Listening chart, and number five in that year's ranking of Top Easy-Listening Singles. "Throughout my entire career," Vikki noted, "my favorite sessions were the live ones, with a live orchestra. To me, that's the epitome of recording. Nowadays, everything is dubbing and overdubbing."

Another thing that Vikki is notable for is initiating a campaign prohibiting smoking during her shows. She was the first performer to speak out publicly against permitting it in Las Vegas showrooms and, although this view wasn't popular at the time, she ended up earning the gratitude of fellow artists and audiences alike. "I was a spokesperson for the American Lung Association for two years," she told me proudly, "and I feel that in a small way, I helped raise awareness of the dangers of smoking."

Recently Vikki was leaving church in her hometown of San Antonio, Texas, when a gentleman and his wife approached her to talk about *For Once in My Life*. As she described it, "The man said, 'That Persian Room record is one of my all-time favorite, favorite favorites. I keep attempting to bring it to church for you to sign, but my wife won't let me.' So, I signed the missalette bulletin for him, 'Live at St. Matthews.'"

. . . .

CONSTANCE TOWERS'S SHOW-BUSINESS career has been a superb blend of extraordinary talent, extreme good luck, and perfect timing.

While still in drama school, Connie was strolling down Fifth Avenue with Ben Lipset, a friend who happened to be a talent agent, when they ran into Pierre Boultinck, manager of the St. Regis Hotel. After introductions, Pierre asked Connie if she could sing. She looked to Ben . . .

"Yes, she can sing," he quickly confirmed.

"Can you open in three weeks at the Maisonette in the St. Regis?" he asked. Another act had cancelled and he needed someone to fill the spot.

And so it began.

On opening night at the Maisonette, Max Arno, head of casting for Columbia Pictures, was so dazzled by Connie's performance that two weeks later she found herself jetting off to Hollywood to sign a contract with Columbia Studios. Her

Bobbe Norris took a turn on the Persian Room stage in the '60s.

movie career was off and running when she costarred with Frankie Laine in Blake Edwards's *Bring Your Smile* (1955).

Young and eager to work, Connie decided things were not moving as fast as she'd hoped in California. She moved back to New York and resumed her singing career, stepping right back onto the stage of the Maisonette. This time, she was spotted by producer Marty Rackin, who pursued her for a film he was making with John Wayne and William Holden, directed by John Ford. (It seems Connie had to be in New York to get the attention of Hollywood.) So back she went to California, for her first big movie, *The Horse Soldiers* (1959), followed quickly by Ford's *Sergeant Rutledge* (1960).

If they'd offered frequent flyer miles in those days, Connie would have cornered the market. After she wrapped the Westerns, in 1961, she returned to the New York cabaret scene, this time performing at the Persian Room.

After a few more movies, she added Broadway credits to her enviable resumé, debuting in 1965 at the Ziegfield Theater in the title role of Anastasia in the musical *Anya*. Connie went on to play Anna opposite Yul Brynner in *The King and I* for an amazing eight hundred shows. She also won the New York Outer Critics Circle award for her portrayal of Maria in *The Sound of Music* in 1967.

But wait, there's more. In addition to the movies, theater, and nightclubs, Connie appeared in countless television shows, even playing leading roles on the soap operas *Capitol* and *General Hospital*. She's guested on *Frasier, Baywatch,*

Criminal Minds, The 4400, Star Trek, The Fresh Prince of Bel-Air, and myriad other television series.

I caught up with Connie, now eighty-nine years young, at the beautiful Beverly Hills home she shared with her husband John Gavin, a businessman, actor, and former ambassador to Mexico. (Sadly, he passed away in 2018.) I couldn't wait to ask her about her wide-ranging career and the stellar success she enjoyed at such a tender age.

"I was around twenty-three when I first played the Persian Room," she told me. "The Plaza was wonderful. It had such glamour. There was a sparkle about that hotel that made you feel good when you were there. My show was basically show tunes, just like cabaret today—Gershwin or Cole Porter or Richard Rodgers. There were four back-up singers and the Ted Straeter Orchestra.

"As part of performing there, you had a beautiful suite where you could entertain people after the show, and I took full advantage of it. I had Joan Crawford over once! It was a Sunday night, and I was planning to go out with my friends, Al and Dorothy Strassard, when the phone rang and a wonderful voice said, 'Miss Towers? Please hold for Al Strassard.'

"When Al got on the phone I said, 'That is quite a secretary you have.'

"'Don't you know who that was?' he said—he was laughing. 'It was *Joan Crawford*, darling!'

"I had just finished making *The Horse Soldiers* and had seen Joan in Las Vegas, at a party. I was so in awe of her, I said to a friend, 'Isn't she beautiful?' I don't know how

Constance Towers was in her early twenties when she first performed at the Persian Room.

or why, but apparently Joan thought I said, 'My, she's gotten older.' Well! I never thought that and certainly would never have said it. Apparently Joan told the Strassards, our mutual friends, that she had been so insulted that I, this young actress, had commented on her age. Later, when we were all in New York, they told me about it and I said, 'My gosh, I didn't say that! Oh, please bring her to my show at the Persian Room!'

"I walked out, and Joan was sitting ringside, wearing a very ornate, very tall orange Balinese beaded hat and matching coat. When my twinkle lights came on, she twinkled twice as much as I did! Oh, she loved being the center of attention. She was on a double date, along with Spyros Skouras, the head of Twentieth Century-Fox. Every time Joan's date watched me for more than a few seconds, she pulled out a cigarette and held it up so that he would have to turn away from me to light it for her. She must have had fifty cigarettes during my show—and this was ringside, where everyone in the room could watch. It was rather fascinating, actually.

"After the show, they all came upstairs to my suite. There was a couch and a chair and she stayed in the corner of the couch and never said a word. She just stared at me. I was standing by the door when they got up to leave. She took my hand and said, 'I have to have tea with you. I have been very mistaken about something. I will call you tomorrow, and my car will pick you up at three.'"

"I didn't have other plans, but if I had, I would have cancelled them because who would miss the chance to visit with Miss Crawford?

"Sure enough, she sent her car—a Rolls-Royce—at the appointed hour, and the chauffeur drove me to her apartment, which was up on Fifth Avenue somewhere in the Seventies. When I arrived, Joan was busy giving an interview, but when the reporter left she showed me around her apartment, a fabulous triplex overlooking Central Park. Then we went downstairs, had tea, and she apologized for behaving so badly during my show.

"I was in awe of the whole experience, but so glad that I finally had a chance to tell her myself what I had said that night we went out: how *beautiful* I thought she was. I guess she believed me!"

Nudging Connie's attention back to the Persian Room, I asked her if she'd had a choreographer for her shows there.

"I had a man by the name of John Gregory who did my shows, and he was a genius—just wonderful. I always relied on him. My shows were about fifty minutes long. I'd always change my gown for the second show and I'd try to change the music as well, or at least the sequence of the numbers, because there were some people who would come multiple times, maybe one night for the first show and another for the second."

After mentioning her gowns, Connie asked if I'd like to see one. What do you think?

These particular gowns, she explained, were designed by the movie director Mitch Leisen and had been commented on by reviewers because they were so extraordinary. They were referred to as *string* or *fringe* gowns and cost around $10,000 in 1961! Connie still has two of them.

"I don't know what to do with them. I can still wear them and hate to just give them away, although I did give the white string gown away. At one point my singing teacher told me about a girl who was opening someplace and needed a gown. I said I have something I think would be right. I gave her that one but I still have the red one and the green one. Let's go take a look."

With that, Connie and I entered the walk-in closet off her bedroom and she showed me the most beautiful dress I have ever seen. I really understand why it was so costly. She explained that each piece of string had to be measured and placed just so to conform to the shape of her body. The dress and all the draping were done with pieces of silk string.

What a perfect ending to a wonderful day.

. . . .

VISITING MICHELE LEE, I found it impossible to believe that almost fifty years had passed since she'd starred alongside Robert Morse and Rudy Vallee in *How to Succeed in Business Without Really Trying*. Michele greeted me at her beautiful Beverly Hills home looking vivacious and fit. She was wearing black tights, a long-sleeved black T-shirt, and ballet flats—as if she'd just stepped out of rehearsal or off the set of her 1969 Walt Disney hit *The Love Bug*.

Michele's television and screen career took many forms and crisscrossed different genres, including roles in Carl Reiner's *The Comic* (1969), in which she starred with Dick Van Dyke and Mickey Rooney, and a TV production of the musical *Roberta* (1969). In 1996, Michele made history when she became the first woman to write, direct, produce, and star in a television movie—*Color Me Perfect*—the story of a mentally challenged woman who is used in a scientific experiment to reverse her disability. Returning to Broadway theater, she received a Tony nomination in 1974 for her performance in *Seesaw*, the Michael Bennett, Cy Coleman, and Dorothy Fields musical adaptation of William Gibson's *Two for the Seesaw*.

But none of that made Michele a household name. That came in 1979, when she took on the role of Karen Cooper Fairgate in *Knots Landing*, a TV spin-off of the popular nighttime drama *Dallas*. *Knots Landing* dominated prime-time ratings until 1993, running an impressive 344 episodes—and Emmy nominated Michele set a record by appearing in every single one.

According to Michele, her entire family was musical. Her father was a Hollywood make-up artist who loved the piano and wrote songs, one of which, "What a Day," was sung by Jimmy Durante.

As a teenager, her brother, Kenneth Dusick, played guitar and dabbled in songwriting, and Michele wrote a few pieces with him. The tradition continues: Kenneth's son Ryan, Michele's nephew, is one of the founding members of the successful rock band Maroon 5.

Squinting in an attempt to decipher titles from the substantial CD collection in her spacious great room, I asked Michele if she always knew she wanted to be in show business.

"My mother always said I sang in my crib," she laughed. "I sang all through school and in junior high I was known as 'the singer.' I started singing quasi-professionally when I was sixteen, with a society band. We performed on weekends, and it was thrilling to get paid for what I'd always done for fun!

"While I was still underage, I lied so I could work in LA at a club called Dino's on the Sunset Strip. As it happens, the building Dino's was located in was used in the hit television series *77 Sunset Strip*, starring Efrem Zimbalist, Jr. My father was Efrem's makeup man on *The FBI Story* and sadly passed away during the series."

I turned the conversation to Michele's memories of New York and the Persian Room. How did she come to perform there, I asked.

"I had an incredible manager, Stanley Kay. Before he was in management he was a drummer for Buddy Rich and he was a brilliant, funny, magical musician. Anyway, he arranged for me to audition at the Persian Room. I had already done *How to Succeed in Business Without Really Trying*, and I think I had also just completed the movie—but I had to audition because I was an unknown quantity outside of stage and screen. That was the real beginning of my singing and nightclub career. I had done a little singing in Los Angeles, but this was big stuff. To sing at the Persian Room meant you'd made it. You'd *made it* in New York!

"My audition consisted of twenty minutes of my act, me and a pianist, and they hired me. I performed there twice—taking my act to the Sands Hotel in Vegas in between."

At that point, Michele's wonderful executive assistant, Tina, brought us coffee—though it tasted more like heaven: freshly ground with foamy, sweet heavy cream, sprinkled with sugar, and accompanied by cinnamon sticks. She also brought us strawberries, grapes, cheeses, and yummy biscuits to keep us going. *Who wants to work?* I thought. I just wanted to sit there and lose myself in Michele's gracious hospitality, while enjoying the view of the golf course and the LA canyons out of her floor-to-ceiling windows.

After a little break, I asked Michele if any well-known people had come to see her perform at the Persian Room.

"Diahann Carroll came. All I remember is that something went wrong; I forgot a lyric or something. She was really hot stuff then—a big star. She was Diahann Carroll and didn't

*Singer and pianist Buddy Greco, who contributed some
of the musical arrangements for Michele Lee's Persian
Room debut, congratulates her after the show.*

have to audition anymore! Knowing she was there must've made me nervous. The notes came fast, and the words came fast, and I got so hung up that I don't think I ever caught up. All the while I was thinking, *Oh my God, Diahann Carroll is out there!*"

When I spoke with Diahann, I asked her if she remembered Michele's flub. " No," she answered quickly, "I don't remember that at all! Michele Lee was always a very strong and interesting performer. She always did wonderful work."

Michele continued telling me who was there for the show. "Jim Farentino was my husband at the time, so of course, he was there. David and Ellie Janssen and Paul and Peggy Burke were our good friends—they were there. David was a huge star because of *The Fugitive*, and Paul was in a hit TV series called *The Naked City*. Other pals who came included Jerry and Marta Orbach, Buddy and Dani Greco, and Harry and Patty Duke Falk. They were all part of our 'gang.'

"Buddy Greco did some charts for my act, just as a friend. I believe the song was "On the Other Side of the Tracks." I think it was my opening number.

"At that time, I was with Columbia Records and had a hit with "L. David Sloane." Those years were all about career, career, and career. Well . . . I guess not completely. I remember trying to get pregnant during my Persian Room run. Talk about working all evening and then up all night! At that time, if you thought you were pregnant, you had to go through this whole test and you waited forever for the results. It didn't happen for us until the following year."

Figuring it might be time to change the subject, I asked Michele about what she liked to wear for her act. It was, after all, a time wen just about anything went, fashionwise.

"I wore some great dresses," she told me, her eyes lighting up, "but one of my favorites was a dressy miniskirt in some kind of shiny gold fabric. I don't remember the designer, but it was sleeveless, with a really cool bronze, hand-beaded and jeweled metal collar. The dress was backless except for very delicate, metal crisscross straps that came from the neckpiece, down below my waist and just above my . . . um . . . you know what. It was very sexy.

"After the show, we'd either entertain or hang out with friends. Many times Marta and Jerry Orbach had everyone over

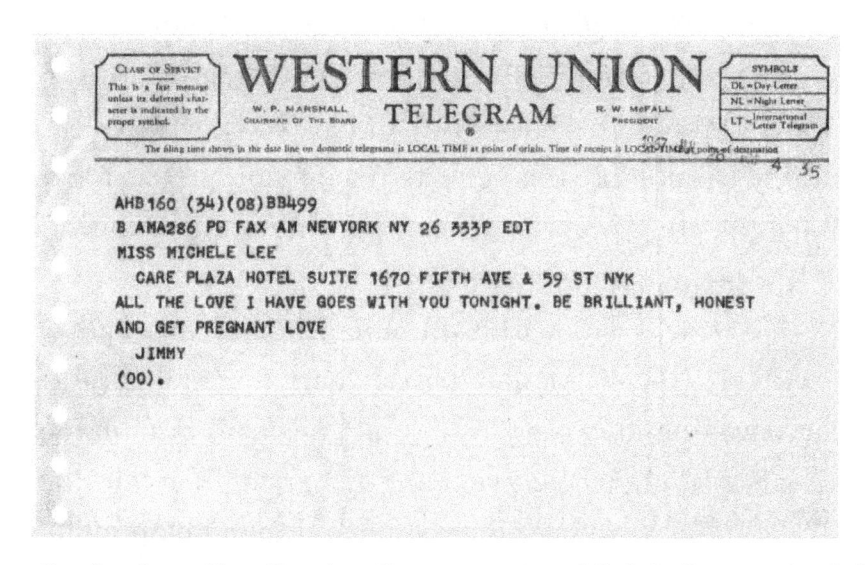

On the day of her Persian Room opening, Michele Lee received this telegram from her then husband, James Farentino. (They were waiting to find out if she was expecting a child at the time.)

to their place. They lived downtown and had a huge wooden kitchen table. Marta would cook and the gang would all sit around, tell stories, eat pasta, and drink wine. Fun times."

．　　．　　．　　．

KENTUCKY-BORN DANCER, SINGER, choreographer, actor, and director Lee Roy Reams is a planner. He'd always wanted and worked toward a career on the stage, but just in case that didn't materialize, he learned shorthand so he'd have a solid fallback. He also earned a degree in English and became a substitute teacher.

"I wouldn't sign a contract with the school because I was only working to save up some money," he explained. "As soon as I had 500 dollars put aside, one of the other teachers drove me to New York."

Another school friend, Marcia Lewis, a nurse at Mount Sinai, suggested that Lee Roy share her little apartment at 96th and Park Avenue. "It was perfect," he gushed. "She worked at the hospital nights, taking care of newborns, and when she got home in the morning, I'd get out of bed, and she'd get in. That's how things were done back then; that bed was never cold."

Lee Roy read about an audition working for Juliet Prowse. "She needed one male dancer for her nightclub act," he explained, "and I got the job. It was my first New York audition and my first job in New York! We took the act to Las Vegas and I was making good money."

I had been instructed to ask Lee Roy about the Juliet version of "Come up and see me sometime," and here's what he said. "Juliet's assistant, Betty, met me at the Las Vegas airport with her Mercedes Benz. She gave me the keys, rode with me to the hotel, and checked me in. Then she told me to see the second show and go to a small party that Juliet was throwing afterwards. I did as she said and after the show I went up to the suite Juliet had for the party. After everyone had gone, I asked her which room was mine.

"'There's only one bedroom here, honey,' she told me.

"*What?* Well, are there two beds in there?

"'No, just one king-size bed,' she said. 'You sleep with me.'

"So I went in and, being a good southern Baptist boy, I put on my pajamas—tops and bottoms—and jumped into bed. Of course, Juliet came out in a gorgeous negligee and said, 'You know, honey, I only sleep in the nude.' *That's OK,* I thought, *I've seen her naked backstage before during the act.* She dropped her negligee, got into bed, and . . . we had a wonderful conversation! Just like two kids.

"'I'm glad you're here, honey,' she said and I gave her a little kiss, rolled over, and thought, *If my friends could see me now!* She was a truly remarkable person. She was gorgeous and absolutely lovely to me until the day she died."

One of their first engagements together was at the Persian Room, and Lee Roy was eager to talk about it.

"Having recently arrived from Kentucky, I was completely ignorant of the Plaza, let alone the Persian Room. Part of the arrangement, it turned out, was a room in the hotel for the duration of the show. Pinch me! I'd landed my first audition in New York—to work with Juliet Prowse—and suddenly I was working the Persian Room and living in the Plaza Hotel! When people would ask me where I was staying, I'd say, quite casually, 'The Plaza.' Honestly, I wasn't putting on airs, I was just dumb enough not to know how that would sound. Understandably, I gained a reputation for being a rich little southern boy whose mom and dad put him up at the Plaza."

One thing about the Persian Room that Lee Roy recalled fondly was Lillian Gaertner Palmedo's exotic murals portraying the pleasures of hunting, dancing, eating, drinking, and singing. These distinctive wall coverings made a deep impression on him, as did other aspects of the experience. "We had four boys in the act, of which I was one of course, and we always had to make adjustments to the show when we were there because, while the room was quite outstanding, the dance floor was small for a dance act. We danced right up to the tables! I'm sure the people at those tables thought we would make them part of the act, but we didn't. Juliet did her famous carousel number, where she held a pole and we were the horses representing the four kinds of love. Fred Ebb and John Kander wrote the act and Ernie Flatt was the choreographer. It was a terrific show, but we couldn't help but sweat a lot. As I said, the space was intimate and all those twists and turns and whipping around sent our perspiration spraying. I remember once someone handed me a dinner napkin to mop my face.

"I quickly came to understand the panache of the Plaza and

how special the Persian Room was. Frank Sinatra attended the show one night and came to the room to congratulate Juliet. You have no idea what a thrill that was. I later went back to see Joey Heatherton with Lauren Bacall as my guest. They had an incredible full orchestra. It was a wonderful time. People dressed up for the evening; men wore jackets and ties—if not tuxedos—and the ladies were in evening dress. It was like being IN the movies. The fact that it was my official introduction to New York City, and that Juliet was my guide of sorts, was incredible. All of it was. I loved Juliet. She was one of the greats and always kept me working."

When that act closed, Lee Roy's next audition was for Bob Fosse's *Sweet Charity*—and he nailed it. But he quickly gave notice when Ms. Prowse insisted that he return to work on a new act with her at three times his current salary! His many other Broadway credits include roles in *The Producers, La Cage aux Folles, 42nd Street, Hello Dolly, Lorelei, Applause,* and *Beauty and the Beast.* His leading ladies—all of whom became dear friends—have included Lauren Bacall, Carol Channing, Dody Goodman, Celeste Holm, Ann Miller, Gwen Verdon, Ruby Keeler, and Ethel Merman. Additionally, he's been invited to the White House to sing for four U.S. presidents. These days, Lee Roy can still occasionally be talked into doing a cabaret show. If you even hear about one in the works, secure tickets immediately. They sell out quickly.

. . . .

GOING OFF TO visit with Tony Butala, the founder of the fabulously popular singing group the Lettermen, felt like a real adventure, so I decided to share it with Sabrina and Marina. After a bus ride from New York's Port Authority to New Jersey, a quick visit with my mother (who loves to pamper all three of us with the home cooking we rarely get in the city), and a visit to the local farm stand for Jersey corn and tomatoes, it was off to Lancaster, Pennsylvania. That's where Tony and the Lettermen—still going strong—were giving a concert at the American Music Theater. Tony had kindly carved out a slice of time to tell me what the Persian Room was like when the Lettermen played there.

As I drove through rural Pennsylvania, watching the beautiful scenery fly by, I was mentally reviewing my notes on Tony and the Lettermen. The three-hour trip passed quickly, and soon I was sitting in the lobby of the Hampton Inn, our meeting spot, nervous that I wouldn't recognize him. Those worries were put to rest when a very handsome silver-haired man stepped off the elevator, only to be enveloped by fans who'd come to town especially for the concert. When the hubbub subsided a bit, I sidled over and introduced myself, and we made our way to a corner table at the cheery hotel restaurant. I knew I'd have to work fast, as Tony was soon due at a sound check with the rest of the group.

He started out the conversation by volunteering his age—seventy! You'd never guess it, believe me.

"I've been with the Lettermen fifty years and singing professionally since 1946—sixty-four years. I still love it," he said. Wow, only six years old when he started. I asked him how that came about.

"Okay, here's the long and short of it, probably more like the long of it. I was five and a half years old, living in Sharon, Pennsylvania, and I didn't want to go to school. The first day, my parents couldn't find me. Eventually they did, two fields over, on top of the highest tree. When they finally got me to go, I clowned around and disrupted the class. I just had too much energy.

"So my mother enrolled me in dance class. I was the only boy with all these girls. In the '40s, ballet was a sissy thing to do, and I got teased for it—but I thought those guys were nuts because even at five and a half I thought girls were great. I was in heaven: thirty little girls and me!

"The teacher had a dance recital to show the parents where their twenty-five cents a month went. As the only boy, I was a star—I played Johnny Jump Up and I stopped the show! Our phone started to ring off the hook: the Moose Hall, the Elks, the Knights of Columbus, the Rotary Club, all asking for little Anthony to do their Christmas Party or Fourth of July bash, and sure enough, I went.

"There seemed to be an aversion to paying kids money. They'd pay the piano player five dollars but give me a set of cuff links or a watermelon in the summer. I was six years old and my mother looked in my little drawer and saw thirty-five sets of cuff links. So we started charging five dollars. Another year went by, and in the second recital I had five numbers. My fee went to ten dollars after that and then fifteen.

Golden moments in Plaza history (clockwise, from top left): Dinah Shore rehearses. The incomparable Hildegarde chats with with Mr. Seay, the Plaza's publicity director, and Mrs. Clarke Williams. Eartha Kitt knocks 'em dead. Ethel Merman chats with Lucille Ball and her husband Gary Morton after her Persian Room opening.

"KDKA radio in Pittsburgh was the first commercial broadcasting station in the world. Once a month, I'd go down there and do the Saturday morning live program. I was heard in Ohio, Pennsylvania, Indiana, Michigan, New York, and many, many other states. So my fame spread, and I was getting calls to do shows as far away as Rochester, New York. I was getting about twenty-five then. That was more money than my dad made."

Enthralled by Tony's story, I didn't notice it at first, but a throng of his fans had gathered at a discreet distance, hoping to catch his eye. We paused briefly so a few could introduce themselves. Tony chatted graciously with Stacey from Detroit, Melva from Cleveland, and others. After a few minutes, he dismissed them gently so he could get back to his story.

"One day, my mother got a call from her cousin in LA. Mary Burke was her name. She had pneumonia and couldn't get her kids ready for school, and her husband was off working on an oil derrick. My sister looked up the train schedule. 'Tomorrow morning, at eight, you can catch the Phoebe Snow from Sharon, and you'll be in Los Angeles in three days and two nights,' she told my mom. My dad said, 'Why don't you take Anthony with you? Maybe he can sing for someone.'

"As it turned out, every fall in L.A., Bob Mitchell had auditions for new kids for his choir. He had to, because they kept growing up and leaving when their voices changed. My cousin Bobby auditioned and was told, 'Don't call us we'll call you.' Then it was my turn. I gave Vince Morton, the assistant director, my charts and started in, trying to hide my nerves. In a few seconds, he got on the intercom and said, 'Bob, you better see this kid now.'

"So, at ten I became a member of the Bob Mitchell Boys Choir in Hollywood. Bob had his own boardinghouse and school, and the kids got paid. My mom cried all the way home, but within two years my family moved out there. I was doing movies and becoming successful."

Hmm, time was passing and we were only up to Tony, age twelve! The truth is, I could've listened to him forever, but I knew I'd better fast-forward to the '60s. We weren't quite at the Persian Room yet, though. The mention of that decade got Tony talking about his good friendship with Sammy Davis, Jr.

"I first met Sammy when I was with a lounge group, Bill Norvas and the Upstarts. We were three guys and two beautiful girls. This was in Vegas, and Sammy would come and watch us after he did his two shows. We had the late shows, 12 a.m. to 5 a.m., and Sammy rarely slept, plus, he liked one of the girls, Laurie Mattis. We had a lot of good times in Vegas. After the Lettermen's first hit, Sammy suggested I take on Jess Rand as my personal manager. It was Jessie who got us the Persian Room, Jess and our theatrical agent, William Morris."

I asked him my favorite question—did he get nervous, especially performing at a swanky place like the Persian Room?

"As a matter of fact, we *were* nervous about playing the Plaza—but Jack Benny—whose TV show we'd been on, and who had taken us on tour—came to our rescue. He happened to be working in New York the week we opened and offered to introduce us. Jack was a big star, and he knew that a place like the Persian Room could make us or break us. No matter how many hits we had, we'd have to have a good show. Well, we knew we had a good show. Peggy Lee and Sammy and all the Capitol Record people said they'd be there, too, which boosted our confidence.

"At the last minute, Jack couldn't make it. Instead, he sent a tape recording of his introduction the morning of our opening: 'Ladies and Gentlemen, I'm sorry I can't be there with you tonight but I'd like to introduce three men who have toured with me and been on my television show. They're spectacular. Ladies and gentlemen—the Lettermen!'

"He managed to get there a few days later and introduce us in person, but for the rest of the run, we used his recording to let people know we had some credentials. I mean, Jack Benny *was* the number-one television star in the world. We came out, well dressed, engaged the audience, sang wonderful songs, and had a great act."

Tony was fully engaged in telling stories and probably could have gone on and on, but I had to insist we take a short break so I could make him some hot raspberry tea. His concert was in just a few short hours, and I wanted him to conserve his voice for all of those adoring fans. When he'd taken a few sips, he continued.

"Judy Garland came to see us at the Persian Room. We had met her when Sammy had us out to Paramount Studios in Brooklyn to tape a special. We tended to hang out at Danny's

Hideaway on Lexington and Fifty-second, where a lot of celebrities went."

Even more than the Who's Who in the audience, I was curious about the act itself.

"We always wore tuxedos. Sy Devore was our tux maker. He made tuxes for Sinatra, Dean Martin, Sammy, everyone of taste. If you had a Sy Devore tuxedo, man—wow. People could tell by the cut. Even though tuxedos sort of look alike, these were the best. I still have them.

"The show was natural in flow and movement. We'd go out into the audience. In those days there were only corded mics, so we had to figure it out carefully: *OK, if I reach the center I pick up another mic and go this way or that way.* And sometimes we'd end up with a lot of spaghetti on stage.

"I didn't want to be the kind of group that was aloof from the crowd. I wanted to tell the audience that after the show we would be out in the lobby signing autographs. Jess said, 'Ah, Tony, I don't think the Plaza will like that.' And I said, 'Why not?' Sure enough, those sophisticated ladies and gentlemen loved it. Our job was to loosen them up, help them relax and enjoy themselves.

"We included audience participation in our act, in the form of a 'camera song.' We'd say, 'Ladies and gentlemen, if you brought a camera along tonight, take it out.' This was groundbreaking—people weren't used to taking pictures during performances. We actually asked people to sing along and have their pictures taken with us. We got one man to be Elvis. We'd get a lady to sing and bump to 'Won't you

Once she's enticed him to come up from the audience, Betty Johnson's brother Kenneth joins her in a duet.

come home Bill Bailey, won't you come home.' We weren't sure this stuff would work at the Persian Room, but you know what? It worked fine! People just want to have a good time. We still do it all in our act today, but we broke it in at the Persian Room in the '60s! In fact, our camera song was so well received that it inspired the Plaza to hire a house photographer to go around and take pictures of couples.

"Those days were just the greatest time in the world. Everyone dressed up. You couldn't walk into a restaurant without a tie. I loved it. Things were more special then. You'd see people enjoying tea in the Palm Court in the afternoon, all the ladies dressed up in their finest outfits and gloves. It was an elegant time. The audience respected the performers, but the performers also had the greatest respect for their audience. You dressed as well or better than your audience because they were paying to see you."

The concert that night was fantastic—it lasted two-and-a-half hours, and the crowd still wanted more. The Lettermen proved they still had magic, closing to three standing ovations!

. . . .

BETTY JOHNSON WAS the one and only performer I spoke to who had a cherished love story to share from the Persian Room. Her name might not be instantly familiar, but Betty was a beloved performer in her day. She was launched into show business as a young child, touring the country and recording albums for Columbia Records with her family, the

Johnson Family Singers. Eventually, she captured the top spot on the *Arthur Godfrey Talent Scouts* show and, with the guidance of Percy Faith, branched out on her own quite successfully.

It was at a Columbia recording session with her family that Betty first met Percy. They were getting ready to sing "The Halleluiah Train" when she noticed a slight man enter the control room and sit down to listen.

"I was curious as to who he was," she explained, "and quickly found out he was a famous Canadian conductor and arranger. He'd just joined Columbia to work with the big names—Tony Bennett and Rosemary Clooney, among others.

"At that initial meeting he presented me with an album of Jerome Kern music he had just produced. I took it home and memorized every single song."

When Betty wrote a note to Percy, thanking him for the wonderful album, he responded with other recordings and became a mentor, helping her craft her style and hone her music choices. He sent her classical albums that developed her tastes in a new direction and offered to help if she ever decided to pursue her solo dreams in New York.

"Percy Faith helped me find and navigate the path I needed to travel," she said. He introduced her to the New York music scene and helped her transition from a southern traditional singer into a popular music performer.

. . . .

AFTER SCORING THE top spot on *Arthur Godfrey Talent Scouts* with her rendition of Irving Berlin's "How Deep Is the Ocean," she was featured for a week on Godfrey's morning show. The exposure she received was explosive and put her on a swift path to the most posh New York nightclubs, starting with an invitation to sing at the Copacabana.

"In 1957, Jack Paar was in the audience when I appeared on *The Ed Sullivan Show*. I sang my hit "I Dreamed," and he told me later that he'd decided to hire me on the spot, but he didn't tell me then because other singers were still auditioning. I got the job and was a regular on *The Jack Paar Show* for four happy years, singing in the first and last segments.

"That exposure brought me many other jobs. That's how I got the Persian Room booking.

"I encountered the love of my life, Arthur Gray Jr., while I was performing in Los Angeles at the Coconut Grove. I dreamed of him every day and was anxious to pursue a relationship, but he lived in New York. The Plaza offered that opportunity. Each night, Arthur was in the audience with a table full of friends, all very attractive people. After the performance he'd ask me over to meet them, and then just the two of us would go to the Oak Room. I was in heaven.

"My dress was white chiffon with a beaded top, designed by Oleg Cassini. I felt very attractive because the lighting in the room was pink and soft and dramatic with a sophistication that most rooms lacked.

"In later years, I didn't perform there, but I did go to the Persian Room as Mrs. Arthur Gray, Jr. On one occasion,

Robert Goulet introduced me by telling the audience we had played together in *Brigadoon* and asked me to take a bow."

Betty passed away in 2022, at the age of ninety-three—but I was fortunate enough to speak with her often before that. At the time, she was mourning the loss of her beloved Arthur, and her tone was wistful. "My strongest memory of the Persian Room is that Arthur and I were in love, not married yet, and he came to hear me sing every night. Of course, I sang every song on the program to him. Afterward, at the Oak Room, everyone knew him, and we had chicken sandwiches and champagne."

. . . .

CATHRYN KENZEL'S STORY is different because she entertained at the Persian Room in 1968, when she was only fifteen years old. "When most people played that room they were already big stars, but my story was different. I was very, very young and the Persian Room gave me my start.

"I started singing at age three and was very fortunate because I had a great gift and two fanatically supportive parents who were thrilled that I wanted to sing. I was brought up in a show-biz family, and they wanted me to succeed as much as I did. They owned Ron-Cris, a recording company. Where most parents would say 'grow up and be a doctor,' no, no, no—with my family it was music, music, music. They handled the Five Satins, and when I was a little kid I met the Four Seasons.

"It was just me and my brother. They were very encouraging and did anything and everything they could to get me a break. You know, network, network, and network, and one person led us to another and to another. Someone led us to Joseph Arcana, who was at that time the president of the New York City musicians union. When my parents met him, I was fifteen and ready to burst out.

"He heard me sing and from that point connected me with a lot of different places and people. The Persian Room gig was the kickoff to the promotion of my record *Other Lips*."

Joseph Arcana was a good friend to have because the unions held a tremendous—*tremendous*—amount of power in New York in the 1960s. On his suggestion alone to the Plaza management, Cathryn got booked. She didn't even have to audition to perform at the prestigious venue.

"I went by Cathryn Rondina at that time, my maiden name. My mother put together my shows, and we opened at the Plaza with 'Get Ready.' It had been done by the Temptations and then Tom Jones. That was my theme song: 'Get ready 'cause here I come.' It was my mother's idea because I was new, I was fresh, I was a kid—and I was ready. I did a lot of Broadway and Streisand songs. I didn't sound like her, but I had a big, belting voice. You could hear me blocks away. At the Persian Room I sang a lot of songs that were powerhouses.

"Vikki Carr was scheduled to appear there the day after I left. She didn't come to my show, but I saw her walk through the hotel. I was so impressed just seeing her. Even at fifteen,

I wanted to be a star. I was terrified and excited. I don't know, though, if I realized the importance of where I was singing at the time. I knew it was important but maybe not as much as if I had been twenty-five. But maybe that was a good thing because I had no fear. Vikki's manager came to my show because someone told him, 'you should go hear this kid who's playing downstairs.'

Cathryn Kenzel was only fifteen years old when she made her Persian Room debut. Here she is with her mother, who put together her shows and traveled with her until she was past twenty; and Tony Bennett, whom she opened for on many occasions.

"There was a man who worked with my parents in Connecticut, and he was so proud that I was going to perform at the Plaza that he bought me a bottle of perfume from Tiffany's as a good-luck gift before I went on. The reason he picked Tiffany's was because the box was the same blue as my dress. That's how I remember my dress color!"

Cathryn told me that her parents traveled with her because she wasn't even old enough to drive. I asked her if the famous Persian Room had lived up to her expectations.

"I've sung all over the United States and in Europe, and I would have to say there wasn't another room that size that was as posh and classy. But that was the hotel. My God, I can't say any place was richer and more elaborate than the

Plaza and the Persian Room. There is no other place that holds the same history as that room."

As Cathryn was just starting her professional career, she didn't have a large following to entertain after the show. Instead, she and her parents would celebrate at what could be called New York City's first theme restaurant: Mama Leone's. "It's closed now but was a famous spot," she recalled. "Now I love Carmines! You can tell I'm Italian. After the Persian Room, my parents traveled with me for about six years."

"I know you sang with many very famous stars. What was it like working with Tony Bennett?" I asked.

"I opened for Tony, and he was wonderful. I remember one day he watched me rehearse a song called 'Let Me Try Again.' If you are a Sinatra fan you know it. It didn't become a big hit, but we loved it. Well, Tony said to me, 'Why are you singing a Frank Sinatra song on a Tony Bennett show?' 'Because you're doing 'I Left My Heart in San Francisco!' I replied. We both laughed over that. He was the most funny, charming, great guy out of all the people I met in show business, very honest and down to earth. He said to me, 'Don't ever be with anyone who doesn't think you're the best thing since ice cream.'

"Rodney Dangerfield was also a very nice guy. He didn't make it until he was older, and I think because of that he appreciated stardom. Maybe you don't as much if you're famous very young and don't have to struggle the way Rodney did. After I opened for him at the Oakdale Musical Theater, he booked me at Dangerfield's in New York."

In her early twenties, Cathryn finally went on the road without her parents. She toured all over the United States and at twenty-six, tired of her gypsy life, she went home to Connecticut, where she met her husband and had her daughter. In 1979, she opened a voice studio in Branford, Connecticut, where she combined both her experience and expertise in music with her love of being a mother. Thirty years later, she is still instrumental in launching young singers' careers.

. . . .

COUNTLESS PEOPLE FAIL to look beyond Connie Stevens's arresting beauty and miss the fact that she is a genuine renaissance woman. She's probably best known for her four-year stint as ditzy nightclub singer and photographer Cricket Blake in the 1960s TV detective series *Hawaiian Eye*, but that was just one credit in a long and impressive career as both a singer and actress. At age sixteen, while still in high school, Connie helped formed a singing group called the Foremost, but her time with them was brief; soon she was ready to pursue a solo career. (The other three members of that group went on to make pop history as the Lettermen!)

After winning a role in the film *Rock-a-Bye-Baby* with Jerry Lewis, she signed a contract with Warner Brothers and became a ubiquitous presence in both TV and movies. She has also been recognized for her tireless efforts on behalf of

The effervescent Connie Stevens, backstage at the Plaza after her opening at the Persian.

America's servicemen. At first entertaining with Bob Hope and the USO, Connie soon struck out on her own to visit and perform at military bases and hospitals around the world throughout the Vietnam and Persian Gulf Wars. For her selfless work and devotion, she was awarded the Decoration for Distinguished Civilian Service by the U.S. Army.

As if acting, singing, and charitable work weren't enough to fill up a few lifetimes, Connie raised two daughters on her own and started a beauty empire called Forever Spring, which she marketed on the Home Shopping Network. The company was such a phenomenal sensation that she was at one point considered one of the top 500 female executives in the United States. She has also written, directed, and produced films and documentaries.

Connie was gracious enough to invite me to her home, just before heading out to Missouri for the premiere of her film *Saving Grace B. Jones*. At my first mention of the Persian Room, she started right in.

"It was—gosh—the late '60s. It was a fun, hip time. I was very young, and the younger crowd was really taking over in places like the Persian Room. If I had to put it into one word, I'd say my act was *athletic*. I was all over that stage. I danced and mimed and sang popular songs. And went from one set right into the next.

"Oh, my God!" she added, laughing as it dawned on her. "I remember the men in my horn section all wore toupees. And I know this because—again—my act was very lively; I moved from this end of the stage to that end and back, and the music was fast and the poor guys were up and down and standing and sitting, playing their instruments. I mean, it was a workout and I was a lot younger than those guys! Well, at the end of the show I looked at them and it was some scene. They were all worn out, with their hair pieces cockeyed and askew! I felt bad for them, but they were a great horn section. Joe Layton put the show together for me, although there wasn't much choreography because the space we had to perform in was pretty small."

I couldn't imagine that she'd done all of that leaping around in an evening gown—so I asked her.

"You're right there. I wore pantsuits. Michael Travis did my costumes, and they were mainly pantsuits.

"Between shows, I usually grabbed a little something to eat and then got a dinner after the last performance. I didn't eat before the first show or do anything special, really; just reviewed the song sequence, did my makeup, and got dressed. Although . . ."—and at this point I saw a strange twinkle in her eye—"one time, I had been busy and didn't do my nails earlier in the day; so I was dressed and ready to go and still had time, and I made the great mistake of polishing my nails. I say great mistake because I was wearing one of my favorite outfits, a black top with feathered bell bottoms. The pants had these fabulously beautiful little black feathers all over. A million black feathers. Well, I was on stage doing my act—all happy—sashaying around as usual, and I looked at my hands and the nails were covered in black feathers! I hadn't given them enough time to dry, and with all the

Connie Stevens met her future husband Eddie Fisher while performing at the Persian Room.

dancing around, the wet nail polish had grabbed the feathers and glued them on. I'm sure that anybody who noticed thought I had done it intentionally—and come to think of it, it wouldn't be a bad idea!

"I met Eddie [Fisher] while I was performing at the Persian Room. We had met before but hadn't gone out because our schedules conflicted. Well, this time we went out, got married, I had my two girls with him, and we got divorced."

Connie had a stroke in 2016, and has mainly kept out of the public eye, but we've visited, and I see her on special occasions. Such as at a concert recently, supporting her good friend Lainie Kazan.

. . . .

LIZA MINNELLI MADE her nightclub debut in 1966 at the Persian Room, and at the time she was just a somewhat shy dancer attempting to add singing and comedy to her repertoire. Lucky for her, she had some special material written for her by Fred Ebb and John Kander, who had written Broadway's *Flora the Red Menace,* in which she'd starred the previous year. Although she started off tentatively, Liza rapidly found her groove when she launched into what became her signature song, "Say Liza." (Most people call it "Liza with a Z," and that became the title of her hit TV special in the '70s.) Liza may have been born in her mother's trunk, but she it was clear even then that she had gifts all her own.

As if Liza's singing and kidding around weren't enough, oh, how she danced—accompanied by two more-than-able-bodied partners, Neal J. Swartz and Bob Fitch. Avi Duvdevani, a longtime devotee of New York City cabaret, recalled how, when he was just shy of eighteen, he visited his first nightclub—to see his contemporary, Liza. As a sophomore at Brooklyn Technical High School, he would often ditch classes to catch a matinee *Flora* at the Alvin Theater, so he was already a fan.

"I had seen over a dozen performances of *Flora the Red Menace*," he told me, "and it was a sad day when the closing notice was posted. But when I read she was appearing at the Persian Room I started to make plans. I didn't own a tux so I went to Alexander's—a dear departed department store—and purchased a sport coat. It was light blue and I had the tailor add some black piping around the lapels. That and a clip-on bow tie made me reasonably presentable."

Avi and his date made a pit stop for a dozen roses on the way to the Plaza from the Number 4 subway. When they arrived at the venue, he immediately asked the maître d' to deliver the flowers to Liza. To this day, he has the card he received from her, thanking him and inviting him backstage after the show. "It was a fabulous night," he recalled, beaming. "That show was the beginning of my life-long friendship with Liza and my love affair with cabaret. I even ate sweetbreads!"

I think of Avi as representative of an entire generation of New Yorkers for whom a rite of passage was attendance at a variety of events at the city's finest theaters, cabarets, jazz clubs, and nightclubs. Today, on any given night, Avi and his lovely wife Marsha can still be found at Birdland, 54 Below, or another of the city's gracious and magical performing arts venues.

. . . .

LESLIE UGGAMS APPEARED on the TV series *Beulah* in 1950, when she was just six years old. By the time she was seven, she was opening at the famed Apollo Theater in Harlem for such greats as the Louis Armstrong and Ella Fitzgerald. She attended the New York Professional Children's School and then the prestigious Juilliard School, all while maintaining a presence on television and stage.

Just shy of age fifteen, Leslie became a contestant on the popular game show *Name That Tune*, where she not only won $25,000 but caught the attention of Mitch Miller. He gave her a spot on his wildly popular show *Sing Along with Mitch*, and signed her to a recording contract. This was groundbreaking: Leslie became the first female singer to join Miller's troupe and one of the first African-American entertainers to become a regular on a prime-time TV show.

Leslie left Juilliard in 1963, making the first of her three appearances at the Persian Room that same year. She was one of the youngest performers ever to play there, and at the time was described as part Lena Horne and part Shirley Temple.

I couldn't wait to ask her how it felt to play the Persian Room at the tender age of twenty.

"The Plaza was such an elegant hotel. I was so young that my mother stayed with me the first time I performed there. During the day, I rehearsed and taped *Sing Along With Mitch*, then I did my show at night. It was an enchanting time—my first nightclub gig, and I enjoyed every bit of it!"

I had to phrase it carefully, but I wondered if young Leslie didn't find the place a little bit stuffy, a little too grown-up?

"Not at all. The room itself was very warm, almost intimate, and the audience was attentive. It was a very welcoming place. This was 1963, and even my Afro-American family was made to feel very comfortable when they came to see me perform.

"The management had such high standards. I was given a beautiful suite for the duration of my stay so I could dress and prepare for my show in pleasant, relaxed surroundings. In fact, I think the Plaza was responsible for my own high standards. I soon found out that talent wasn't treated that way at other nightclubs.

"What really stands out in my memory is that I was hired to perform there on New Year's Eve. The original plan was for my family to come watch the show and ring in the New Year with me afterwards. I also invited a few—anyway, it seemed like a few—other people who didn't have previous plans to join us. Well, word spread, and it became a huge party. My suite was so packed we had to open the door and people stood around in the hallway. Millions of people! I didn't even

Look out for the sweet young sting!

It's Leslie Uggams. And she has it. And what's more, she's going to prove it in front of everybody in the Persian Room from December 18 until January 7. She's quite a bombshell. When she sings, firecrackers go out of style. She smiles and... what's the use. You'll just have to see for yourself. And speaking of spectacles, Rome is *way out*. Emil Coleman's Orchestra and Mark Monte's Continentals are *in!* For reservations, please call PLaza 9-3000. And for a very lovely evening, visit the Persian Room.

HOTEL CORPORATION OF AMERICA **THE PLAZA**

Leslie Uggams made her television debut at age six, so by the time she debuted at the Persian Room at age nineteen, she was a very pretty veteran.

know a lot of them. I actually walked into my bathroom and found two complete strangers making out in my bathtub! All in all, though, it was a wonderful party. For years and years, I'd run into people and they'd say 'I remember that great New Year's Eve party you had at the Plaza.'"

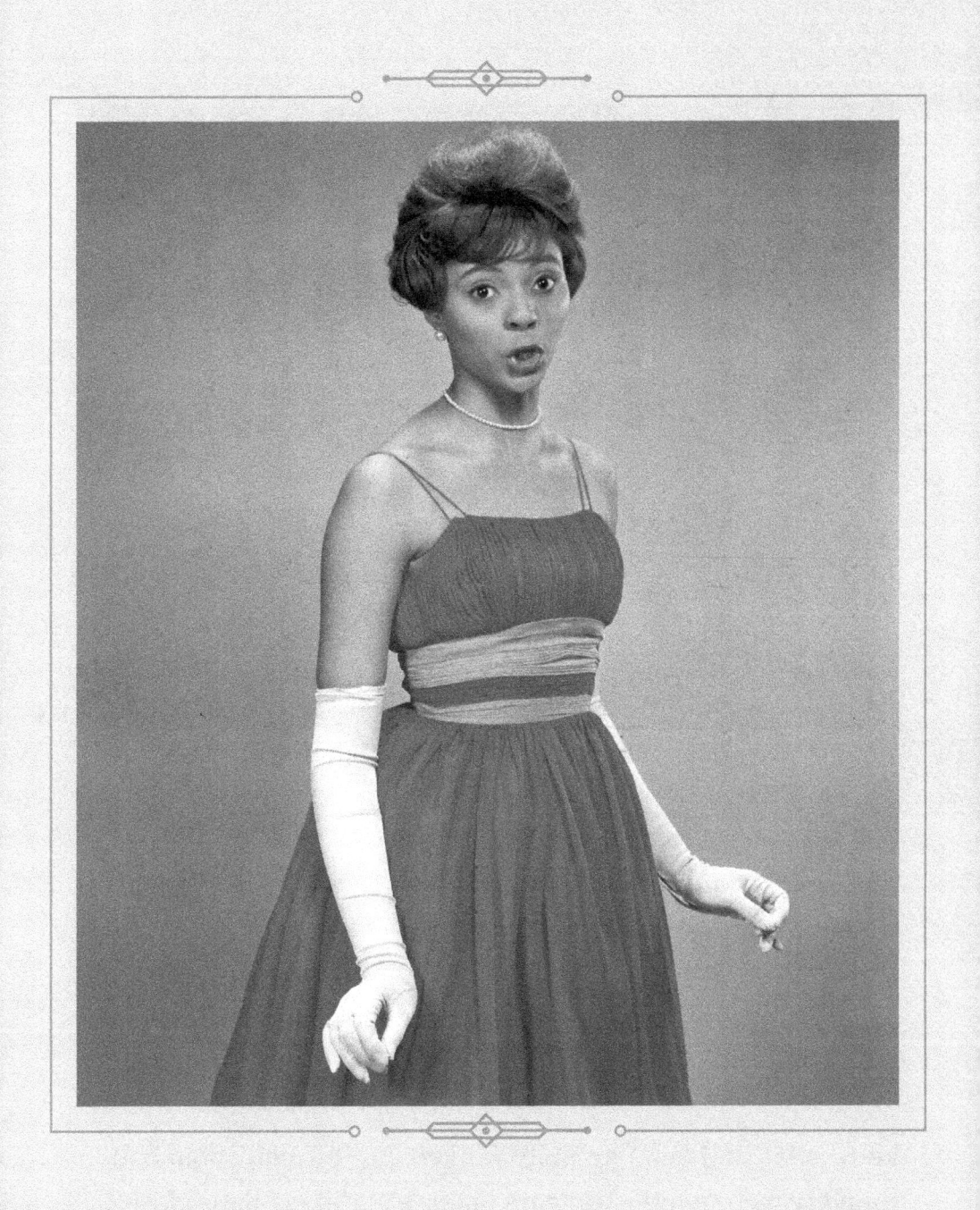

Shortly after her appearance at the Persian, the wonderful Leslie Uggams was tapped to star in her first Broadway Musical, Hallelujah, Baby!, *which catapulted her to stardom and a Tony Award.*

In 2013, Leslie portrayed Lena Horne in a musical bioplay called *Stormy Weather*, and she continues to perform concerts around the world. She is active in Democratic causes and occasionally voices characters on animated TV series, including two episodes of the hilariously irreverent *Family Guy*.

. . . .

TONY SANDLER USES a variety of words to describe his childhood years in West Flanders with his father and seven siblings: innocent, peaceful, playful, and charming. Tragically, that would end when Tony was just seven years old and Belgium surrendered to Germany. Returning home after fleeing in a panic with only a few belongings, the family found their farmhouse damaged but still standing. Only days later, a German soldier moved in and stayed for the duration of the four-year occupation.

When the war finally ended and life returned to normal, Tony was invited to sing with an international choir and his life-long love of performing was born. His first recording, at age eighteen, was a Belgian seventy-eight single called (in translation) "The Song of the Sea." Many more records followed and Tony's popularity soared.

After serving in the army in Korea, Tony resumed his performing schedule and quickly became a celebrity, his smooth, romantic sound rapidly endearing him to European and English audiences alike. But it was the Café Roma, on the Italian Riviera, he considered his home base for five years. While appearing there, the American producer Frederick Apcar persuaded him to team up with the American singer Ralph Young. The next stop for the duo was the Casino de Paris show at the Dunes Hotel in Las Vegas.

Ultimately billing themselves as Sandler and Young, the two singers soon caught the attention of Phil Silvers, who told his audiences in the main room, "I don't know what the rest of you are doing now, but I'm going to the lounge to listen to that hot new duo, Sandler and Young."

I'll let Tony take it from there.

"At around the same time, Polly Bergen saw our show and asked us to flank her at the Desert Inn in Las Vegas. In 1965, we were traveling with her when she took her show to the Persian Room at the Plaza! That was a big deal to us. By this time Ralph and I had performed in many places, both separately and as Sandler and Young, but the Persian Room had a worldwide reputation of class."

The Persian Room announces a 28-day cruise with Tony Sandler and Ralph Young, who will be duo-ing what comes internationally from October 18 till November 14. Ports of call include faraway lyrics with sweet sounding names. Burt Farber and Mark Monte will help you sail around the dance floor.
For deck chairs, PL 9-3000.   THE PLAZA
HOTEL CORPORATION OF AMERICA

Tony Sandler and Ralph Young's first appearance at the Persian Room was in the company of Polly Bergen—but by 1966, they were headliners playing to sold out crowds.

Naturally, I had to talk to Polly Bergen about it. When I asked her about the fact that Sandler and Young were the only performers she ever shared a stage with, she said, "They were *definitely* not backup singers. They were very talented guys. I saw them and felt I just had to have them with me. So I brought them on and they were a big asset. I thought of them as part of the act and used them that way. They did their own numbers, and then we did numbers together. They were wonderful."

Handing Tony back the mic: "We had a fabulous time in Polly's show. After that, we toured on our own, and a year later, in 1966, we were back at the Persian Room but this time it was *starring* Sandler and Young, and to sold-out houses!"

. . . .

PERHAPS WE HAVE Patti Page to thank when we're stuck in snail's-pace traffic along scenic Route 6A through Cape Cod. Such is her power as a singer that her renderings of "Old Cape Cod" and "Tennessee Waltz" have had a demonstrable impact on home sales and tourism in Massachusetts and Tennessee! In 1967, Massachusetts House Speaker John Davoren and Treasurer Robert Crane presented her with an official State Citation for the contributions to that state's economy. "Tennessee Waltz" had sold more singles by the mid-1960s than any previous song.

Although Patti was getting ready to leave for a concert tour to the Philippines when I first caught up with her, she was kind enough to invite me to her picturesque Rancho Santa Fe home to discuss memories of her nightclub years. After a delightful house tour that included a stroll through her office, where scores of platinum and gold records were on display, we sat down to talk.

I told her that "Old Cape Cod" had always been one of my favorite songs. "Mine too," she admitted, perhaps not surprisingly. "Claire Rothrock wrote the song, and she lived on Cape Cod. She and the gentleman who published it came to see me when I was playing Blinstrub's in Boston. He played it for me, and I fell in love with it. We made arrangements to go to New York City the very next day and record it."

Knowing that Patti's time was precious, I got right down to business, and asked her how many times she'd played the Persian Room. "Three different times," she told me. "I remember once the Plaza was in the middle of a major spring cleaning. Everything was being polished and refurbished.

Patti Page received a set of doorknobs from the Plaza as a gift, after she joked that it was kind of them to welcome her with her own monogram on the doors!

The hotel manager was showing me around, and we walked into a room that was empty except for piles of doorknobs and switch plates that had been removed and stacked for cleaning. They all had that familiar PP monogram beautifully scrolled on them. I joked to the manager that they didn't have to go to the trouble of putting my initials on the doorknobs! And, wouldn't you know it? The sweet man had one mounted and he presented it to me before I left. You might have noticed it when we went through my office. I still display it.

"My engagements at the Persian Room were a bit different from other people's. I didn't get the crowd that usually goes to the Plaza, you know, the upper-crusty clientele? My audience was classy but not typical. They were a little more country, more hip, and younger.

"I always wore white on stage because no matter what kind of lights they have in a club, white shows you off well, and you can do a lot with it. That was one of my then-husband Charlie O'Curran's contributions to my act. He also staged it for me—he was a choreographer. He incorporated a glittering, mirrored disco globe overhead that reflected all the lights.

"By the time the show was over, it was midnight. I always ate after the show. Room service at the Plaza ran twenty-four hours a day, so I'd order dinner sent up to the room. It wasn't like when I played Vegas. After the show there, I'd have dinner and then play tennis—until 4 a.m., sometimes. You know, when you're young, you don't even think of the time.

I'd go to bed at five, get up at one, and start all over."

Maybe I was getting a little tired of hearing every artist rave endlessly about the Plaza; I asked Patti if she'd had any less-than-perfect experiences there.

"Well, this wasn't the Plaza's fault," she replied, "but there was a giant snowstorm one of the times I was there, one of the worst the city had had in quite a while. Then again—it really turned out for the best. A lot of people staying at the hotel were stranded inside for days with nothing to do, so they came to see my show. The same people came over and over and over. A lot of the employees had to stay, too, and they came to hear me sing. I had packed houses.

"There are certain feelings you get in certain rooms in New York City, and you just know it's the place to be. The Persian Room was one of those rooms. It lent itself to the show and had a warm feeling to it. Plus—it was right next door to Bergdorf's!

"I had five musicians in addition to the hotel orchestra, a hairdresser, sometimes a secretary, my manager, husband—quite an entourage, and that was before I started bringing the kids along. And the management was nice to all of them."

Sadly, Patti passed away on New Year's day 2013, at the rich age of eighty-five. But her tribute to Cape Cod remains deep in the heart of all New Englanders and those of us who love to vacation there.

. . . .

Patti Page played the Persian Room three times, and drew a somewhat younger and hipper crowd than some of her fellow artists.

CAROL LAWRENCE BECAME famous for her dazzling Broadway portrayal of Maria in Leonard Bernstein's *West Side Story*. She cemented her reputation as a singer and dancer starring in many, many Broadway shows, including *Sugar Babies*, *I Do! I Do!*, and *Sweet Charity*.

In addition to being a star of the first magnitude, Carol is one of the most gracious women I've ever met. She had just returned from a tour and had plans for the evening, yet she made time to visit with me on a Sunday afternoon. Not only that, but when I arrived at her stunning home I was greeted with a tempting array of treats: chocolates, exotic nibbles, delicate Italian cookies that I couldn't stop myself from finishing, and sweet hand-squeezed lemonade.

Both Carol and I thought our conversation would be shorter than it was—but when she started replaying events, I noticed a relaxed, playful look take hold behind her eyes. She really enjoyed reminiscing about her New York City nightclub adventures! Carol made it to her evening soirée on time—but with very little to spare.

I started out by reminding her that Ed Sullivan had called her Persian Room performance the greatest nightclub act he had ever seen.

"That was the headline, and the next day you couldn't get in," she remembered. "We were sold out for the whole run!

"I always say Tony Charmoli, my choreographer and friend for many, many years, was the king of making ladies look great onstage. My act consisted of two boys—Johnny Harmon and Bobby Lane—plus me and a ten-foot-high ladder. (Kaye

Carol Lawrence shares a joke with her then husband, Robert Goulet

Ballard is emphatic in claiming the ladder act came about because Carol is so petite that she required a lift. Whatever its origin or reason, it was a huge hit!) I like starting a show 'in trouble.' It started dimly lit, with two spots going gangbusters, searching . . . like in Dick Tracy. The music was unidentifiable. Our backs were to the audience and I was dressed as one of the boys because we were pretending that one didn't make it to opening night. The tuxedo purposely didn't fit me well—the sleeves came below my fingers. My long black hair was up under a derby hat. Finally, the orchestra leader said, 'Here she comes . . . bop, bop, bop. Here she comes . . . dat, dat, dat . . . Missss Carolll Lawrrrrence.' We were on our knees looking upstage, and the spotlights converged on an empty space. There was a hush as the audience wondered where I was.

"I was playing Johnny, and at this point, Bobby would take my hat off and my hair would fall out. 'What are you doing in Johnny's tuxedo?' he'd ask.

"I'd say 'You know how Johnny is always late for everything? Well, he's late for opening night! And Mr. John starts the show at eight whether I'm here or not. So I figured I'd just dance his part and sing my part until he got here.'

"He said, 'Do you think it will work?'

"I said, 'We don't have a choice. Hit it maestro!' And we began the song 'I'd Do Anything' from *Oliver*. Right then, Johnny came in, and gave this wonderful excuse for being late—that he was calling his mother. She lived in Florida and he was a real mama's boy, so the whole premise rang absolutely true. I pretended to be all annoyed and said, 'I don't want to hear any more excuses, let's start from the beginning.' I handed him his derby, and the orchestra started the intro again, while I ducked behind a little black velvet curtain where my secretary ripped off the velcro tuxedo. Underneath it was my white leotard, over which I put a fabulous chiffon Ginger Rogers skirt, a beaded jacket—and ran back on! I said hi and started my first number and the whole change took less than thirty seconds.

"We didn't have an opening act. The show was one hour, ten minutes. I told Tony, 'You really choreographed this for Sonny Liston, but he's not here and I'm dying!'"

I asked her about her most memorable experience at the Persian Room, and her eyes lit up.

"My biggest thrill was . . .Well, Mr. John always gave me

a list of who would be in the audience, so I could point them out. He'd say, 'You must introduce him first and then this one, because he will get angry if he's not first' And on and on. He knew everyone so well. He got tips from all the celebrities to put them at the best tables.

"This time he said, 'Tonight . . . tonight, tonight, tonight, you are so lucky. He seldom comes, but guess who's here? Cary Grant! But you are not allowed to mention his name because he will not stand up. He will sit at the table closest to the door by my station. He doesn't want to be mobbed. He will not sign autographs. Tonight he is a private person.'

"All during the show I saw people walking and moving around and finally I realized what it was. Women would go all the way across the room to the powder room because they spotted him. They would just stare at him all the way over and all the way back. At least they weren't asking for autographs, because if they tried, Mr. John would step in and say, 'No, you are disturbing the show; you must move on.' He really ruled the place.

"So, on that particular night I introduced everyone else in the audience and then—I just couldn't stop myself. I said, 'and of course everyone in the audience knows there is an elephant here who cannot be introduced, but he needs no introduction. I have been a great fan of his from the time I can remember.'

"Cary stood up. 'Well, this just doesn't happen!' he said and I thought he was furious! He folded his napkin—I thought he was going to leave—but he walked to the front and the audience just stood. He came on stage and HE KISSED ME!"

"He said, 'Miss Lawrence . . .'

"My knees really almost buckled. I said, 'You are absolutely gorgeous,' in my best Fanny Brice voice.

"'Well, thank you, my darling, and right back at you,' he twinkled. The audience was blown away.

"After the show he came up to my suite and talked with us for an hour. My two backup boys just sat on the floor awestruck. Before he left, I took him aside and said, 'Tell me your secret. You're not twenty-nine anymore but you sure look it. Your skin is exquisite; tell us just one of your secrets.'

"'Well my darling,' he said, 'I sleep a lot. Make sure you get enough sleep.' Oh, he was adorable—such an aura about him.

"The only one to come close to him was JFK. I had lunch with him at the White House. I was in the Oval Office just two days before he was killed, for a press conference kicking off his reelection campaign. Lena Horne was there and a lot of people from Broadway.

"Lyndon Johnson had seen my act at the Persian Room, but I wasn't allowed to introduce him either, for security reasons. He sat in the corner and loved the act.

"We were all going to do a big, big show for the start of his campaign. I was the first of our group to go into the president's office. He shook my hand and said, 'Lyndon tells me you have the greatest act in the world. I can't wait to see it at Madison Square Garden.'"

As big a star as she was, it must've felt pretty special to have the president looking forward to your act. And the loss must have felt devastating—even moreso than for the rest of us, if that's possible.

Ed Sullivan called Carol Lawrence's Persian Room act the greatest he had ever seen.

Other Persian Room performers from the 1960s:

Ed Ames	Gogi Grant
Nancy Ames	John Gary
Susan Barrett	Tammy Grimes
The Barry Sisters	Sam Hamilton
Shirley Bassey	Noel Harrison
Cilla Black	Florence Henderson
Xavier Cugat	Fran Jeffries
Vic Damone	Kitty Kallen
John Davidson	Alice and Ellen Kessler
Johnny Desmond	
Sacha Distel	Abbe Lane
Phil Ford and Mimi Hines	Julius LaRosa
	Denise Lor
Sergio Franchi	Gloria Loring
Jacqueline François	Dorothy Loudon
Robert Goulet	Grace Markay

Tony Martin
Gail Martin
The McGuire Sisters
Barbara McNair
Ethel Merman
Matt Monro
Phyllis Newman
Bobbe Norris
Russell Nype
Jane Powell
Katyna Raniere

Felicia Sanders
Dinah Shore
Frank Sinatra
Kay Starr
Enzo Stuarti
Caterina Valente
Monique Van Vooren
Shani Wallis
Izumi Yukimura
Florian ZaBach

CHAPTER SEVEN

The 1970s

Peter Duchin follows in his father's footsteps at the Persian Room piano.

It was in the '70s that we said goodbye to Elvis and witnessed the breakup of the Beatles, yet no other decade saw the launch of more diverse musical styles and artists. We enjoyed heavy metal, soft rock, punk and pop, and thrilled to the ballads and pop tunes of Stevie Wonder, Billy Joel, Marvin Gaye, and Elton John. But the single, decade-defining craze in music was sparked when John Travolta pointed one finger skyward, resplendent in his iconic white suit in *Saturday Night Fever.*

Disco was born, and the country couldn't get enough of the sounds of Donna Summer, the Bee Gees, Gloria Gaynor, and KC and the Sunshine Band. The new sound influenced fashion as well as song and dance: platform shoes, polyester leisure suits, hot pants, Spandex tops, gold and white suits that glowed under ultraviolet lights—all became wardrobe staples (on Saturday nights, if not at the office). For the first time in a century, big, bushy sideburns were cool on men. African-Americans proudly displayed huge, round Afros and other natural styles. Farrah Fawcett popularized the feathery haircuts that began replacing the long, straight, center-parted hair of the '60s.

Enormous auditoriums and arenas such as Madison Square Garden that could accommodate multitudes of screaming fans became homes for the ground-shaking rock-and-roll performances of the Rolling Stones, Led Zeppelin, the Eagles, Pink Floyd, Chicago, Aerosmith, the Who, and many others. Nightclubs, cabarets, and supper clubs began to fade in popularity, though the flame never went out completely.

Although plagued with crime and the threat of bankruptcy (bailed out at the eleventh hour by the Teachers Union), it was in New York City in the mid '70s that some of the country's most groundbreaking music emerged. That said, the Persian Room greeted the decade like an elegant, aging dowager. In an effort to remain competitive, the supper club abandoned big, sophisticated, star entertainers backed by full orchestras and turned its talent selection over to outside bookers. Other local clubs, most notably the Maisonette at the St. Regis, were there to pick up the slack. The Maisonette quickly enticed orchestra leader Burt Farber to move his home base there, and along with him went some of the sophisticated dazzle that had been the Persian Room's hallmark.

But the Plaza's management hadn't survived for nearly seventy years by being blind to its own missteps. A year and a half later, they reversed the new policies and quickly revived the Persian Room's air of chic sophistication. Challenges remained—mainly attempting to determine just what style of entertainment its audiences now craved. In this revolutionary decade, did patrons want to hear show tunes, comedy, dance music, folk, pop, rock-and-roll, American standards? It would take a bit of trial-and-error to figure it out how to keep the club relevant (and its velvet seats filled) while maintaining the traditions that had made it special in the first place.

Time waits for no one, but the Persian Room soldiered on for another half decade, showcasing the finest entertainers of the moment and offering a haven for its loyal patrons. And when it did close its doors for the last time, it was with its usual grace. The moment was mourned by many—including the greats who had performed within its walls—as the end of an era.

. . . .

JUST PRIOR TO meeting me at New York City's Regency Hotel, Lainie Kazan had returned from a trip to England where she visited with friends, had dinner at the House of Lords, and met the Queen at Windsor Castle. I was under no illusion that she would be anticipating our little get together as eagerly as I was, but she seemed genuinely happy to sit down with me and share the American imitation of high tea.

I had to begin by asking her about her audience with the Queen.

"The whole thing was so surreal," she said, her eyes sparkling with the memory. "We were briefed on how to address her—'Your Highness,' of course—and how to curtsy. She had a brief conversation with each of us. Nothing very important; just weather and stuff. But she drove herself down in a little car, and came onto the lawn to meet with us."

Lainie had her first huge taste of stardom when, after being Barbra Streisand's understudy in *Funny Girl* for over a year, she got her chance to shine as Fanny Brice for two precious performances when Barbra contracted strep throat. Her reviews in the local press and national magazines were glowing, and Lainie's career was launched.

Over the next almost fifty years, Lainie captivated audiences worldwide as a singer, performing in the finest clubs, concert halls, and Las Vegas clubs. As an actress, Lainie received a Golden Globe nomination for her performance in Richard Benjamin's film *My Favorite Year* and a Tony nomination for the Broadway musical adaptation of the same show. She even picked up an Emmy nomination for her guest spot on the TV show *St. Elsewhere*.

There's lots more to say about Lainie's long and varied career—including the fact that she was the inspiration for Jack Kirby's DC comic book heroine Big Barda—but the point here, after all, is to talk about the time she spent at the Persian Room. The day after Lainie's SRO opening there, Robert Alden reported in the *New York Times* that "an audience may have many reactions to Miss Kazan, but they

Lainie Kazan looks positively dangerous in this early publicity photo.

will not ignore her." I wondered what had led her to that particular venue.

She warmed to the topic immediately. "I had very recently left *Funny Girl*, and my manager got me into the Plaza. They gave me a summer date because they didn't know if I'd bring in the business, and they were taking less of a risk in summer, when there are fewer people anyway. They didn't pay me much at the beginning.

"After that first booking, I was there three or four times a year for months at a time. Eventually they gave me a suite for the entire year. Anytime I wanted to come to New York I would stay there. It was gorgeous. I had never seen anything like it in my life. They were unbelievable to me. I had the suite Elizabeth Taylor had shared with Richard Burton.

"The club was very intimate. Even though it held 250 people, it felt smaller. I remember it always being packed. People would stand in line for hours to get in. It was so elegant. On one night alone, in my audience, were Cy Coleman, Ethel Merman, and Joan Fontaine. After the show I'd have friends over to my suite for a glass of wine. We'd sit around or go out to another club. Liza [Minnelli] would come over, and we'd go out. Places were all open very late. I partied hearty—I was like a werewolf!"

"I thought after my Persian Room experiences that everything would be like that. Ha!"

I asked her about what she wore for her performances. "Great, great gowns," she told me "made by Ray Aghayan, Bob Mackie's partner. This one gown made me look—at a glance—like I was nude, but I wasn't. It was the color of my skin, had a jeweled buckle, and graced my legs with chiffon. It was gorgeous. I also had many other incredible clothes. I still have some of them in a big trunk.

"Oh, and that reminds me of another story," she said, laughing as she remembered it. "One of my trunks was an enormous thing that had once belonged to Sophie Tucker. Really, really huge. I bought it at a place called Jimmy's Trunks on Ninth or Tenth Avenue. It was black and looked like a coffin. It opened, had a pole, and all my gowns would hang in there. And I carried my own sound system with me, along with my trunks. I used to make the doormen and bellmen carry all this stuff to my suite. They'd have to open all the double doors just to get it through. They would see me coming and they would die—that's how I traveled—with the trunks and speakers. Big speakers. I didn't like their sound system so I carried everything. "OH, NO, she's coming,' they'd say."

I knew that Lainie had performed at the Persian Room in both the '60s and '70s, and I wondered if she'd noticed the club changing with the times.

"Well . . . here's one thing that happened in the '70s that could never have happened in the early days of the club. My girlfriend Cynthia was married to a guy, Steven Friedlander, but he called himself 'Brute Force' because he was against the Vietnam War and everything establishment. He wrote songs that were way out of the box—very edgy, very outrageous songs that I thought were brilliant. At one point I

*Liza Minnelli and her new husband,
Peter Allen, join their good friend Lainie
Kazan after her opening-night show.*

said to him, 'Steven you have to open for me at the Plaza.'

"I don't know if you can write this, but I'm going to tell you because it's one of the great stories of the Persian Room. Eartha Kitt used to come in a lot, and she was there the night that Steven performed. She had come with Liza. All the singers were there. Well, Brute Force walked onto the stage with his loose, bright red hair flowing halfway down his back. He wore tails, high-top sneakers, no tie, and he sat at the piano and started to sing."

I think I'll spare you the lyrics Lainie repeated to me, but suffice it to say they were not from the common cabaret lexicon!

"The audience just gasped. Paul Sonnabend, the owner of the hotel, was hysterical. He said to my manager, 'Get him off that stage or she's out of here!!' And we had to fire him. Steven was hysterical—very irreverent—but this was the '70s and I thought his act was great. I could never invite him back though, because they threatened to fire me if I did."

When I asked Lainie if there was anything she missed from those days, she didn't have to think long. "I miss the elegance," she said, "and the dress code. People got all dressed up to come hear you sing. They respected what you were doing. They'd eat and drink before the show—never during it—and when you were performing nobody moved! The show was the SHOW. There was always great regard for the artist. I really miss that. When you go to a venue now, some dippy waitress is serving ringside and you want to kill her. They don't even know what they're doing wrong.

"The Persian Room had a great staff, and we had great, great times. That roomed sizzled. It sizzled!!"

. . . .

It's my party and I'll cry if I want to,
Cry if I want to,
Cry if I want to. . . .

The lyrics to Lesley Gore's chart-topping hits swirled nonstop through my head for days leading up to our get-together. She was a singer, songwriter, and the most successful solo artist of the "girl group" era. Her first hit, "It's My Party," went to number one on the pop charts while she was still a junior at the Dwight School for Girls in New Jersey. She soon became a platinum-selling pop singer with hits such as, "Judy's Turn to Cry," "You Don't Own Me," "Sunshine," "Lollipops and Rainbows," and "Bobby's Girl." She also had villainous fun playing Catwoman's evil assistant, Pussycat, on the *Batman* television series in 1967. All this, while simultaneously studying drama and literature full-time at Sarah Lawrence College in Bronxville, New York.

We met at a very good seafood restaurant called Fulton's (now departed) on the Upper East Side of Manhattan. It was a picture-perfect day, so we decided to have lunch outside on a small, sunny patio ringed by lush green potted trees.

I asked her to tell me the first thing that came into her head when she thought about the Persian Room.

"I recall the stage being on the floor level," she said. "You weren't higher than the audience. I really played to the tables. There was a small platform for the band. I say 'band' but it was really an orchestra. I had a rhythm section with ten horns. Another thing I remember about playing the Persian Room was that they didn't have a spotlight. It must have been out of order or something. We needed a dress rehearsal to calculate which ceiling light worked for which songs. After marking the perfect spot, I had to remember to stand exactly there when singing a specific ballad. That was a big deal at the time—a big pain."

I told Lesley that she'd always impressed me as being very calm, very "go with the flow," and asked her to corroborate.

"Well Patty," she said, leaning in for emphasis, "you have to understand that I was just a kid and didn't really expect or plan on my degree of success. Quincy Jones heard me sing and said I should make a record. So I thought, 'sure, whatever, let's make a record.' This is a story that's been told before, but it really exemplifies the time. A more uncomplicated time. Back then, we would book a studio and turn out a record in a day. Now, you're lucky to get it done in a month. Anyway, we recorded 'It's My Party' during the day, then Quincy hosted a party that night and got to talking with Phil Spector. Phil told him that a group he was managing, the Crystals, was going to record the best song he ever heard: 'It's My Party'!

"Quincy immediately figured out that we had been 'double dealt' by the publisher. There were two partners; one sold us the exclusive rights and the other sold them to Phil Spector! The next day—Sunday—Quincy went to the studio and pressed one hundred copies of our version. It took him all day, but he was able to mail them out on Monday to the biggest radio stations across the country, we preempted Phil's record. Three days from start to distribution! Try that today."

When I asked her how she passed the time when she wasn't performing or recording, Lesley smiled mischievously and said, "I had an apartment in New York City but rarely stayed there. I was dating a new guy, so it was more exciting to stay in the room the Plaza offered rather than either of our apartments. We spent a major portion of my free time in that suite with room service. It was a lot of fun."

It's my party, I couldn't help thinking.

"I vaguely remember that the cover charge at the Persian Room was twenty dollars," she continued. "Or maybe twenty-five. It wasn't very expensive compared to today. There were a ton of wonderful people in my audiences. I remember Mayor Wagner came one night, so did Diana Ross, Barbra Streisand, Lainie Kazan, Trini Lopez, Little Anthony, Liza Minnelli—those are just a few that jump to mind. It was an awesome place that pulled people in. People came no matter who was performing. I'm sure my name brought in certain fans, but the room itself brought people who just loved to come.

"One of the things I loved about playing there was that I could try new material. I wasn't just a rock-and-roller, you know; I was interested in jazz and other kinds of music, and I put it all into my show. I had the opportunity to do songs other than my hits, and that was satisfying for me. That's what entertainment is about. It was a wonderful experience, possibly one of the best performing experiences I've had. I always thought the Persian Room was really the ultimate in clubbing."

Until a diagnosis of lung cancer cut her career short, Lesley continued to sing, write, and perform. She snagged an Academy Award nomination for cowriting the Top-20 hit "Out Here on My Own" for the soundtrack of the 1980 film *Fame*, starred in the 1995 Broadway musical *Smokey Joe's Cafe*, and entertained millions at a variety of venues around the country. She passed away in February of 2015 at just sixty-eight years old.

· · · ·

KAYE BALLARD, WHO left us in 2019 at the beautiful age of ninety-three, was a star of stage, television, and nightclubs. She performed at the White House for President and Mrs. Ronald Reagan, at the London Palladium for the Royal Family, met Mother Teresa, and (she'd want me to add) saw Marlon Brando naked.

Kaye celebrated her thirtieth year as a performer at the Persian Room in 1975, liberally weaving memories of those three decades into her act. It was an ebullient journey to be sure, and a great reminder of what a consummate and skillful entertainer she had always been. For those of you not up to speed, Kaye was a quadruple threat—comedienne, actress, musician, and singer—and on that special night, all of her talents were on display.

Beginning with a few brash quips, Kaye segued into a dexterously delivered flute solo. (She was equally adept at the tuba, but told me she'd thought that might be a "bit too cumbersome" for the Persian Room.) After raucous anecdotes from her storied career and personal life and an array of perfectly selected musical material, she ended with a medley of Irving Berlin songs, accompanied by her long-time pianist Arthur Siegal. Needless to say, she captivated her audience with what Hal Prince once called, "a huge set o' pipes and a delivery that is impeccable." The only talent that wasn't on display that night was her gift for adroit and unerring impressions. (Anyone who watched the TV game show *To Tell the Truth* undoubtedly remembers Kaye's impersonation of Bette Davis—which actually fooled a few of the panelists!)

In reviewing that historic evening, *New York Times* columnist John Wilson enthused, "Miss Ballard is a comedian with a sharp sense of timing. A singer with vocal reserves that can rival Ethel Merman's brassy tone. A musician and actress who can project a sentimental attachment to her Italian grandmother so convincingly and winningly, that it becomes an unstoppable climax for her act." He concluded by saying, "Miss Ballard's talents and most important, the warmth of her personality and the believability she projects, even in the midst of clowning, holds it all together."

I was afraid my first meeting (of what would become many, many visits) in 2010 with the multitalented entertainer,

The hilarious Kaye Ballard began in New York nightclubs such as the Bon Soir and the Blue Angel, working her way up to the big time at the Persian Room with her mix of music and comedy.

a first-generation Italian, was off to a treacherous start. I'd chosen Cuistot, the best classic French restaurant in Palm Desert, California, and when Kaye inquired about their pasta dishes, the waiter informed her they didn't serve any. Luckily (for both of us), the chef graciously whipped up a delicious plate of farfalle for her. As we waited for it, a parade of well-wishers drifted up to our table, and Kaye was uniformly kind to them, chatting and patiently signing scraps of paper.

When the last of her fans had walked away happy, I broke the ice by asking a general question about her favorite venues.

"Oh, I was always busy somewhere," she replied. "I was at the Blue Angel, the Bon Soir, and I also did a good deal of television: *The Doris Day Show*, *The Mothers-in-Law*, and a bunch of others. But that's not what we're here to talk about, is it?"

She was clearly as eager as I was to get to the subject at hand.

"The Persian Room was very different from nightclubs today—that is, the few clubs that are still around. The room was fabulous, and the clientele very elegant. You could tell they took time preparing to go out. Thought was put into what to wear, and the women didn't have a hair out of place. There was an air of sophistication that you just don't see nowadays.

"But, I have to say, the room had the worst ventilation and circulation. Those were the days of chain smoking, and the club was cloudy. Really thick clouds. I've never seen so much smoke. Some nights it looked like I was crying, my eyes teared so much. But everything else was great."

When I asked her if anything out of the ordinary had happened to her there, her eyes lit up.

Kaye Ballard traveled to her Persian Room engagements with her toy poodle, Carmella—who was treated as royally as any other guest at the Plaza.

"That's easy. And it involves my dog."

That got my attention.

"As part of my remuneration, I received a room at the Plaza. I kept my toy poodle, Carmella, there with me."

The Plaza is and has always been pet friendly: dogs, monkeys, tigers, and bears, oh my—but that's another book.

"After my first performance, I ran to my room to check and see how my baby was. And she wasn't there! I was frantic and searched up and down the corridor on my way for help. Spying the house detective I ran to him for assistance, told him my story, and was so upset I didn't even notice that he had Carmella calmly walking behind him on a leash. He said that someone had complained about a barking dog and he was sent to check it out. He felt sorry for my lonely pooch so he decided to take her on his rounds with him. I was so relieved that I let him take Carmella out on patrol with him the entire time I was there."

As a dog-lover, I was charmed—but there was so much else that I admired about Kaye. "Career-wise you have really done it all," I gushed. "You've appeared on the cover of *Life* magazine, for heaven's sake, performed in shows around the world, starred on Broadway and in TV sitcoms . . . is there anything you'd still like to accomplish?"

"I want a Tony," she admitted, "but the Tonys are all political, and I've never been good at playing politics. I'm too blunt. Ask me a question and I'll give you my honest answer. No filter. Maybe it's because I started performing publicly at seventeen and have never stopped. Even during the early and lean years, I never had to take a job outside of show business."

Driving Kaye home, I couldn't help but think that while she might not have received a Tony—yet—she did have another impressive honor. There is a street in Rancho Mirage, California, named after her: Kaye Ballard Lane.

[Old Page 187]

And, if something I mentioned earlier tickled your curiosity, you'll just have to read Kaye's book, *How I Lost 10 Pounds in 53 Years*, to get the scoop on Marlon Brando.

. . . .

ROSLYN KIND STARTED out in show business when she was still in high school, doing demonstration records for her sister Barbra Streisand's publishing firm. After school she went to the studio and recorded songs that the company would turn into demos to send out to performers who might be interested in them. She was fourteen when she started studying dance with Luigi Lewis in Manhattan, where she rubbed elbows with many Broadway gypsies and dancers from *Hullabaloo* and other pop-music TV shows.

"I lied about my age and didn't tell them I was still in high school," she admitted when we sat down to talk. "Two o'clock and the school bell would ring. I'd leave, get my leotard, and take dance class till—oh my God, after ten at night. Then I'd go home, get a bite to eat, and start my homework around midnight."

I'd heard that Roslyn's first engagement at the Persian Room was also her New York debut, so I asked her about it.

"Yes, my New York debut. But before that, I did a lot of other things. My television debut was on *The Ed Sullivan Show*. From there, I played the Hungry i in San Francisco and went on tour for my first album, which was released by RCA. Then I performed in Puerto Rico, Oklahoma, Houston, and on and on, working on my act, all building toward the Persian Room. My act was written for me by Richard Maltby, Jr., and David Shire, the guys who wrote *Ain't Misbehavin'* and lots of other great shows. Some of the greatest arrangers were brought in. Lee Holdrege did my first album and Jonathan Tunick, Harold Wheeler, and David Shire were my arrangers.

"I turned nineteen while I was at the Persian Room. I remember that one critic wrote that I brought, 'a youthful essence never known to that room.' I did songs from *Hair* and *Promises, Promises* because I was young and wasn't going to do older songs. I was a little bit out of whack, with a whole different energy than they were used to. I was determined not to do stuff someone else was known for. Also, being so young, I didn't want to sing about heavy things like loss of love, because I hadn't experienced that. *When I Fall in Love* was actually the only love ballad I did—and it was a hopeful one—except for things that were on the charts or special material that David Shire wrote for me.

"I had a medley of 'I Dig Rock and Roll Music' and 'I Get By with a Little Help from My Friends,' and something we called the Sunday medley, consisting of songs from the '40s,

'50s and '60s. It included 'Sunday Kind of Love,' 'Sunday, Sunday, Sunday,' 'New York Sunday,' and others."

At that point Roslyn started singing softly, and the people around us stopped what they were doing to listen. The Beverly Hills restaurant where we sat is accustomed to welcoming celebrities. As I glanced around, I could see the servers and guests alike realizing that they were being treated to something very special, but they were all respectful and let Ros do her thing undisturbed.

"David, Richard, and I would go to the music store," she continued, "the Colony, and pick out sheet music. We spent days picking and sorting through material. I did 'Sunday Will Never Be the Same,' a hit for Spanky and Our Gang, and another hit on the charts, 'Will You Be Staying After Sunday?' Each one was from a different decade, but they were all about love. I didn't have any backup singers; it was just me and the Persian Room orchestra, plus my own key men: my accompanist, drummer, bassist, and lead horn. Seventeen pieces in all. I can tell you what the ad in the paper said: 'Roslyn Kind is what you get for being good: December 17 through January 6.'

"I loved the maitre d' there, what was his name . . . Frank?"

I reminded her that it was John. Mr. John.

"Oh, my God, yes. He was a doll. Every night he gave me a pep talk. There was one night that Bette Davis was in the audience. Actually, I'm in one of her biographies. It seems that the gentleman she was with that night said, 'Oh, look Bette, Roslyn Kind is performing.' And she went, 'Who?' 'Barbra's sister.' 'Oh, right.'

Roslyn Kind with the creative team for her Persian Room debut, including Broadway songwriters Richard Maltby Jr. and David Shire, seated on either side of Ros.

"I remember that night clearly. Mr. John told me that Miss Davis was in the room and that I should be sure to introduce her—she loved to be introduced. Well, according to her book, that wasn't exactly so. She said I put her on the spot with that introduction, but she stood up and blew kisses to everyone anyway. I'll never know the truth."

I reassured Roslyn that from what I understood, Mr. John never got it wrong. To change the subject I asked her whether her early shows differed from her late ones.

"Yes," she said, "well . . . usually. I'll tell you about something that happened when I was working out of town, getting ready for the Persian Room. One night, while I was working at a club called the CopaHavana in Oklahoma City, a big fight broke out. These drunk guys had stayed for both shows, and when they heard the same songs in my second show they got very pissed. We told them we were trying to break in a show for New York and we had to do this material as much as possible. They were just not having it, and a big Western-style brawl broke out. I swear, people were flying over the banisters and over the bar, and my musical director signaled me to leave the stage by a different route. These guys were so rude and uncontrollable that we had to call the police.

"Afterward, I saw my manager. He had been hit in the nose and his glasses were broken. He told me not to tell his wife what had happened. I had to laugh. 'You won't have to say a word,' I said. 'She's going to take one look at your face and she'll know!' Thank God, in New York we had maître d's like John to keep the weirdos at a distance."

I asked Ros whether the Persian Room had lived up to her expectations.

"My vision of the Persian Room turned out to be exactly right. I had gone there to see . . . I think it was Lena Horne. So I had the gist of what it was. As I said, I was a little worried because I knew I had a younger act. But I couldn't let that get in the way. I still had to be me.

"As nervous as I was, it was all very exciting. I'm not sure whether I felt more confident afterward, but maybe . . .

accepted. More like I belonged. It was an accomplishment to play the Persian Room, especially so early in my career."

I had delicately been avoiding any discussion of Ros's megastar sister, but eventually, she brought up the subject.

"Things kind of got out of hand as I was starting my career. Originally, people weren't supposed to know who I was related to. I needed the time to develop as a performer without the comparisons. Then I did *The Ed Sullivan Show* and someone from my record company leaked it out. After that, I had to 'evolve' in full sight of everybody.

"The Persian Room wasn't like the little clubs, the ones in the Village where you started without the rigmarole. This was major press and major people wanting to come and see and gasp. I had to live up to a lot of things I wasn't ready to live up to. My show there was an incredibly important event for me. I felt my career was riding on the reviews I'd get. I remember a review that said, 'Clearly this teenager's star is rising like a Saturn rocket.'"

When I asked Roslyn how she spent her days during the run, she simply said, "I slept late." I could only assume that meant late nights out after her shows—but where?

"We would hang out at the hotel and have dinner. I never ate before a show—I couldn't. People would come up and visit. On opening night you would have thought my room was a funeral parlor there were so many flowers! I'm from Brooklyn, down to earth. To this day, when I'm on stage, I'm on; and when I'm off, I'm off. On stage, I'm more cocky and confident. At Carnegie Hall, I took off my shoes on stage,

Roslyn Kind backstage after her 1969 debut at the Persian Room, being congratulated by her half-sister Barbra Streisand.

and that was before my sister ever did it in her concerts. Nolan Miller loaned me a pair of shoes for my gown and my toes were dying. I didn't think, 'Oh, this is Carnegie Hall, I can't do this.' And the funny thing is, people actually thought it was part of the act. I got laughs.

"Another time, sequins from my gown started falling off as I was singing. So I picked them up and asked if anyone had a bag to put them in. The audience was hysterical. I'm a very informal type of human being.

"Someone once asked me, 'what's the difference between working a small room and a major venue?' I said the trick is to make the humongous room feel like a small intimate room. That's my job. That's why I'm there—to make everyone feel that warmth personally. The Persian Room actually showed people my potential. It introduced me to the world. World-class critics for world-class papers and magazines covered me there. It was important. My sister's movie *Hello, Dolly!* was scheduled to premiere the same day as my Persian Room debut, and she made her studio move it to the next night so she and my mother could be with me on opening night."

. . . .

THE ACTOR AND singer Jean-Paul Vignon was born in Ethiopia of an Italian mother and French father, studied in France, but was influenced by anything American. That included movies, but especially music. According to Jean-Paul, he listened to every Frank Sinatra record he could find, but whatever his secret, his unique background gave him universal appeal. In France, he won a singing contest and a manager, and that provided structure for his career. He began singing in cabarets, recorded for Barclay Records, was eventually featured in two movies, and lots of television shows.

But I'm getting ahead of myself. After a mandatory break for military service, Jean-Paul decided he needed a new start—a re-introduction of sorts—so he worked his way to New York on the cruise ship *The France* by entertaining its well-heeled passengers. Pleased to find that his act appealed to the Americans on board, the ambitious young man went immediately back to Paris to close up his apartment, sell everything superfluous, and embark on a new life in New York City. He made his debut there at the Blue Angel, opening for a young comic named Woody Allen.

Talent is key to success, of course, but a little serendipity never hurts. It turned out that Jean-Paul's girlfriend and Mrs. Ed Sullivan shared a hairdresser. Long story short, Mrs. Sullivan prevailed upon Mr. Sullivan to send scouts to catch Jean-Paul's act, which landed him an audition and eventually eight appearances on the star-making show. That, in turn, got him signed by Columbia Records and invited to sing on *Merv Griffin* and other variety shows. Soon, he was guesting on non-musical television series too, including *Columbo, Murder, She Wrote, L.A. Law*, and others. He even made a couple of movies! That's what I call talent-plus-serendipity.

During the 1970s, Jean-Paul took a turn on the Persian Room stage, where he offered a mix of tried-and-true American and French standards.

"Americans at this time equated France with sophistication and glamour," he told me when we got together "The Persian Room crowd just ate up the French songs I did, as well as those from the American Songbook. The era of big bands had pretty much passed, but the band at the club was still sizable and just terrific. They followed my charts for the French songs without a problem, which I can't say every band was capable of doing.

"I remember I did the Gilbert Becaud French hit 'What Now My Love?' and it was a huge success. In fact, if I dared to leave it out one night, I'd hear about it later. It is a beautiful song, and because of how it was received by the swank Persian Room audience, I told my guys at Columbia that I wanted to record it. They didn't like the idea! They said it might be good for a supper-club stage, but not a record. Of course, soon afterward, both Herb Alpert and Sonny and Cher recorded the song and had big hits!"

"Americans loved everything French in those days, and the Persian Room audiences were no exception; we were always sold out. I have so many memories of performing there, but one fact stands out: the place had the best of everything. The band was top notch, the cuisine, ambience, everything was great. Even the lighting was superior, which may seem like a small detail but the fact that I remember it fifty years later, I tell you the lighting engineer was a stand-out. The end of 'What Now My Love' goes 'What now my love, now there is nothing, only my love, goodbye.' I had my hand outstretched, and the spot zoomed right in on it before going out. It was very visual and dramatic, and the audience loooved it."

Jean-Paul met Farrah Fawcett playing tennis at Merv Griffin's Mulholland home, but didn't think about her again until after his show had opened at the Persian Room. On opening night, he was introduced to a fan who wanted to invest in him and finance a new recording. Something about the conversation made Jean-Paul think of Farrah, and the fact that she'd expressed interest in working with him. They ended up singing the song "You" as a duet, with Jean-Paul singing in French and Farrah whispering the English translation.

Unfortunately for Jean-Paul, soon after they recorded the song Farrah became a huge TV star on the hit series *Charlie's Angels*. Her agents and managers felt it best to keep her fans focused on the "angel angle" of her celebrity and squashed the release of the record. It was a minor setback for a truly international star who went on to enjoy a rich and varied career.

Jean-Paul currently resides in LA and can be heard on many American films dubbed into French. Lots of Americans have heard him, too—whether they realize it or not—as one of the voices in DreamWorks' *Shrek*.

. . . .

SABRINA AND MARINA settled in with me at my favorite San Clemente beach breakfast spot, the Bagel Shack, to visit with Jack Jones. They promised to share an egg bagel and sit patiently on the comfy, wicker sofa on the outdoor patio while Jack and I visited. At the time, he was busy putting the final touches on his new CD but had graciously carved out some time to call in from his home in La Quinta.

I'd been longing for an opportunity to talk to Jack, one of the most popular vocalists of his time—and a very busy one I might add—for over a year, but his busy schedule hadn't eased up until recently. It was worth the wait.

Jack, born John Allan Jones, is the only son of actress Irene Hervey and singer-actor Allan Jones, best remembered for acting the straight man in the Marx Brothers films *A Night at the Opera* and *A Day at the Races*, and for his chart-topping hit song "The Donkey Serenade."

After signing a recording deal with Capitol Records while a teenager, Allan invited his son to join him on stage for his engagement at the Thunderbird Hotel in Las Vegas. This was Jack's first professional gig. They sang duets, including "The Donkey Serenade," and then he sang a solo, his first in front of such a sizable paying audience, and he liked it.

Capitol Records and Jack soon differed on the direction in which his music should go, and they parted ways. He found that the progressive record label Kapp was a much more compatible match. The first song he recorded for them, "Lollipops and Roses," snared Jack a Grammy for Best Pop Male Vocal Performance. It was swiftly followed by "Wives and Lovers," which earned him another Grammy and a spot at the table with the big boys: an engagement at the Persian Room!

Jack Jones greets his biggest fan—his mother, actress Irene Hervey—after his Persian Room debut.

Jack entertained sold-out audiences many times at the Plaza, starting with that first appearance in December 1964 and continuing through October 1975.

"That was my debut," said Jack. "I was scared to death and excited at the same time; I had hit the big time and had hardly paid any dues at all.

"John Springer was my PR guy, the top PR guy in New York, and he handled the opening, doing a marvelous job. Everyone was there. Leslie Caron was going with Warren Beatty—they were both there—and, of all people, I forgot to introduce them! Warren was a friend and he kiddingly gave me trouble over that for a while.

"Ethel Merman was there, and yes, I did remember to introduce her. She stayed a good friend of mine throughout the rest of her life. So many people were there; it was a real star-studded audience.

"That entire time surrounding my first successful opening at the Persian Room was so exciting. Just prior to it, I'd been playing a tiny club called the Living Room, so it really happened quite quickly.

"There's a funny story about that initial success. Peter Leverson worked for John Springer, my PR guy, and one day we were sitting around my suite talking on the phone, doing PR stuff, and Peter called the hotel operator for something—I don't remember what—but I heard him say, 'Operator, enough, enough. I'm talking to you from Jack Jones's suite, and I want you to X-Y-Z. . . .' When he hung up, I remember saying to him, 'Peter, it appears that my newfound fame has gone to your head!' And we both had a good laugh."

I had read John Wilson's *New York Times* review in preparation for our chat and I reminded Jack how complimentary it was.

"Yes, thanks," he replied. "*Billboard*'s was also pretty good. I remember another time there," he continued. "I got a call in my suite from the maître d', John, who was a real character—very European, and he knew what to do and how to handle everything. One of his tasks was to keep tabs on who was coming to the show. So this particular night he called and very excitedly said, 'Mrs. Kennedy is coming in! It's wonderful!' I agreed that it was great. So they pulled out the best china the Plaza had to offer. There were amazing flower arrangements. Her table was especially beautiful, and the staff is polished everything, right down to their last coat button.

"Then John started calling me saying, 'Jack, you have to hold the show, she hasn't shown up yet.' Okay I said but let's hope it's not for too long; I don't want the other people getting mad at me."No, no, no, it will be fine,' he said.

"He called me two or three times more with updates, basically that she still wasn't there. 'OK,' I said, "but I can't hold the show much longer.' I went downstairs and just waited, keeping a lookout from behind the swinging door to the kitchen.

"Finally, John came and told me she'd canceled. *How can she do this to me?* I thought. Ah, well. Even though I never had a chance to meet her, she was reported to be a big fan.

These things happen—you hope they don't, but they do—and you just have to roll with them.

"During one of the early years at the Persian Room, I was doing a show and a woman was sitting ringside with her back to me. After a while it started to drive me nuts. I kept trying to get around and look at her but she never looked back. In fact, she kept shifting to keep her back turned. Today I would have understood immediately what was what, but I didn't get it then.

"I got really frustrated, but I said to myself, OK, just get through the show get off the stage, and start looking forward to the late show. I ended the show, went upstairs, relaxed a bit, came back down, heard the introduction and applause, and thought, *great, this show will be fun.*

"I went out, and the same lady was still there. She'd liked it so much she'd stayed for the second show—still with her back to me! I finally figured out she was probably blind and enjoyed the music more when she was positioned a certain way."

"I wouldn't have figured that out even today," I said. It seemed we'd exhausted Jack's supply of performance anecdotes for the moment, so I switched to another favorite subject of mine. "What did you do during the day to keep yourself busy?" I queried.

"Oh, I was busy. Kapp Records wasn't too far from the hotel, so I'd go down there and get on the phone with the DJs, which was something wonderful we did back then—communicate with the people who were playing our records. Now it's iTunes and satellite radio, which are also good, but

Crooner Jack Jones after his Persian Room debut in 1964, with a diehard 18 year-old fan in Liza Minnelli.

it was different then. Now I host an hour on satellite . . . that's what radio is now. You don't have one hot DJ."

"Not like when we had Wolfman Jack and Casey Kasem," I say, wistfully.

Jack is very much the gentleman and has made a practice of not discussing his wives and girlfriends. "It's not germane to the story," he'd explain. I agreed with him, but I have to share one little tidbit because, after all, he told it to me—and it's cute.

"Did your wife or girlfriend—depending on the year—attend any of your Persian Room shows?" I asked.

"I think my ex-wife, Jill St. John, might have been there at some point when I played that room . . . wait a minute . . . she was. I remember this because we used to go around the corner to the jewelry store, Van Cleef & Arpels!" (What a surprise to have a man's memory jogged by shopping!) "We also enjoyed the Palm Court."

"One of my appearances was videotaped, and this particular time my dad was there. I introduced him and got him up for a song with me, which was something I didn't want to do because he'd really been drinking. He was a recovering alcoholic, and he eventually mastered it well, but at that time he was slipping. We sang 'The Donkey Serenade' together, which went just fine. But later when I looked at that video, boy, you could see the apprehension on my face and in my eyes."

More than forty years after his last performance at the Persian Room, Jack is still doing what he loves to do—singing to standing-room-only audiences around the globe.

During the '60s and '70s Jack was a staple on all the popular TV variety shows as well a guest star on the most widely watched TV shows of the day. One of his most recognizable songs is the catchy theme song for *Love Boat*. I wanted to ask him if that was his favorite song, but I felt guilty about pressuring him to soldier on without giving his over worked, raspy desert voice a chance to relax and return to the smooth crooning sound we all treasure. I would hate to be accused of being the reason his CD didn't wrap on time! Sabrina and Marina had scarfed down almost two full bagels, so it was definitely time to wind it up.

Other Persian Room performers from the 1970s:

Edie Adams
The Burgundy Street Singers
Lana Cantrell
Judy Carne
Lisa Carroll
Jimmy Damon
Rodney Dangerfield
Daniel and Damon
Eddie Daniels
Rick Daniels
John Davidson
Vivienne Della Chiesa
Peter Duchin Orchestra
Billy Eckstine
Ethel Ennis
Errol Garner
Kelly Garrett
Donna Harris and Margie Carr
Joey Heatherton
Florence Henderson
Ann Hilton
Marilyn Johnson
January Jones
Frankie Laine
Abbe Lane
London Lee
Diane Leslie
Barry Levitt Trio

The Luv Machine
Gisele MacKenzie
Charlie Marina
Al Martino
The Mills Brothers
Cavril Payne
Kenny Rogers
John Rowles

Ran Sanz
Doc Severinsen
Sis and Gary
Dusty Springfield
Enzo Stuarti
Jack Wilkins
Roger Williams
Karen Wyman

EPILOGUE

The Persian Room staff was always ready to treat guests with tender loving care.

In 1974 the United States entered its worst recession in forty years. New York City suffered from high crime rates, financial disasters, declining city services, and the exodus of close to one million people. Even the famed Radio City Music Hall with its spectacular Rockettes was only a hair's breadth from closing its doors after almost fifty years.

Carol Lawrence theorized to me that a major contributing factor to the nightclub era's demise was the danger of New York City streets during that time. Club- and theatergoers feared for their safety; they stopped going to the kind of shows (like those at the Persian Room) that typically started at 11 p.m. Hotels and cabarets that counted on two shows per night to make a profit were reluctantly forced to limit performances and sadly, eventually closed their doors.

Tony Butala suggested another possible reason for the downfall of great rooms such

Partners in crime (and research assistants on this book), Marina and Sabrina.

as the Persian Room. "They had a house orchestra and the musicians union kept raising the pay scale for their guys, as well as dictating how many musicians had to be hired at a given venue. None of the clubs could afford it.

"The acts themselves also started to think twice. Why play an intimate room where they had to do two shows if they could get paid what the huge concert halls were offering for one?"

Or maybe it was simply the end of an era.

The Plaza Hotel shuttered the Persian Room in 1975. The stars went on to work elsewhere and reinvent their careers. Today the Champagne Bar and Rose Room occupy the space. New York City is prospering these days, though we've had our ups and downs in the intervening years. Let's face it—nothing can really get us down!

Sometimes, when I'm sipping my cocktail at the Champagne Bar, among a sophisticated crowd clad in what passes for formal attire these days (crisply ironed blue jeans, open necked shirts, a tunic over skin-tight leggings), I catch a whiff of perfume mingled with smoke and hear the giggling whispers of the spirits that once performed here, along with the warm applause of those who came to revel in the glamour. Then I catch a glimpse of a little girl peeking around a corner, her jumper and ponytails in disarray, a mischievous smirk on her jam-caked mouth. There is no stage at the Plaza today—but that doesn't mean the magic is gone.

INDEX

A
Abbott, Mame, 37
Academy Awards, 48, 51, 56, 78, 89, 99, 176
Adams, Edie, 100, 242
Adderley, Julian "Cannonball", 85, 106, 110, 112
Aghayan, Ray, 210
Alda, Robert, 47
Alden, Robert, 208
Allen, Gracie, 100
Allen, Peter, 68, **212**
Alton, Robert, 74
Ames, Ed, 200
Ames, Nancy, 200
Anderson, William "Cat", 113
Anka, Paul, 66
Apcar, Frederick, 188
Apollo Theater, NY, 121
Arcana, Joseph, 173
Arden, Jan, **65**
Arden, Toni, **65**
Armstrong, Louis, 108, 112, 115, 122, 183
Arno, Max, 144
Astaire, Fred, 34
Avedon, Richard, 81

B
Bacall, Lauren, 159
Baker, Josephine, 95
Bailey, Ozzie, 110, 113
Ball, Lucille, **163**
Ballard, Kaye, 79, 195, 217-218, **219**, 220, **221**, 222-223
Barrett, Susan, 200
Barry Levitt Trio, 242
Barry Sisters,The, 200
Barry, Fred and Elaine, 59
Basie, Count, 100
Basile, Frank, 50-55, 57, 58
Bassey, Shirley, 200
Beatles, The, 140, 205
Beatrice Kraft and Her Dancers, 100
Beatty, Warren, 236
Becaud, Gilbert, 100
Becke, Eve, 27
Belcher, Ernest, 34
Ben Cutler's Orchestra, 59
Benjamin, Richard, 208
Bennett, Michael, 151
Bennett, Tony, 64, 170, **174**, 175
Benny, Jack, 165
Bergen, Polly, 86-88, **89**, 90-92, 107, 188, 189
Berle, Milton, 37, 122
Berlin, Irving, 99, 131, 133, 171, 218
Bernstein, Leonard, 194
Berry, Chuck, 66
Bill Norvas and the Upstarts, 165
Billy Williams and the Chordettes, 98
Black, Cilla, 200
Blackwell, Richard, 98
Blue Angel club, 219, 220

Bluthner, Julius, 46
Bob Grant Orchestra, 59
Bob Mitchell Boys Choir, 164-165
Bogart, Humphrey, 32, 66
Bon Soir club, 219, 220
Boone, Pat, 66
Borge, Victor, 59
Boultinck, Pierre, 144
Brando, Marlon, 217, 223
Brice, Fanny, 198
Brooks, Mel, 85
Bruce, Carol, 59
Brynner, Yul, 146
Buckmaster, John, 59
Burgundy Street Singers, The, 242
Burke, Paul, 155
Burke, Peggy, 155
Burns, George, 100
Burton, Richard, 14, 210
Butala, Tony, 161-167, 247

C
Cantrell, Lana, 242
Capitol Records, 166, 234
Capote, Truman, 92
Carlyle Hotel, 123
Café Carlyle, 73
Carne, Judy, 242
Carnegie Hall, 105, 123, 338
Caroll, Lisa, 242
Caron, Leslie, 236
Carr, Margie, 242
Carr, Vikki, 141-144, 173

Carroll, Diahann, 66, 92, **93**, 94-96, **97**, 98-99, 129-131, **132**, 153, 155; daughter, 97-98
Carson, Mindy, 100
Casazza, Yolanda, 24
Cash, Johnny, 66
Cassini, Oleg, 177
Chambers, Paul, 85, 110, 115
Champion, Gower, 32, 34, 35, **36**, 37, 38, 48
Champion, Marge, 32-35, **36**, 37-39, 48, 49
Channing, Carol, 66, 100, 160
Chaplin, Charlie, 34
Charisse, Cyd, 34
Charmoli, Tony, 194
Clark, Dick, 98
Clark, Sally, **25**
Cline, Patsy, 66
Clooney, Rosemary, 170
Cobb, Jimmy, 85, 110
Coconut Grove, Los Angeles, CA, 35, 171
Coleman, Cy, 151, 210
Coltrane, John, 85, **116**, 106, 110
Columbia Records, 85, 106, 107, 109, 111, 112, 155, 169, 231
Columbus and Carroll, 59
Como, Perry, 32
Copacabana, NY, 171
Costa, Don, 92
Coward, Noel, 85
Cox, Wally, 100
Craig, David, 38

Crane, Robert, 189
Crawford, Joan, 32, 147-149
Crosby, Bing, 32, 56, 74
Crystals, The, 215
Cugat, Xavier, 200

D
D'Angelo, Pierre and Anna, 100
Damon, Jimmy, 242
Damone, Vic, 200
Dangerfield, Rodney, 175, 242
Daniel and Damon, 242
Daniels, Eddie, 242
Daniels, Rick, 242
Danny's Hideaway, NY, 166
Dario and Diane, 27
Davidson, John, 200, 242
Davis, Bette, 56, 127, 218, 225
Davis, Clive, **132**
Davis, Miles, 85, 96, 106, 108-113, 121
Davis, Sammy, Jr., 130, 165
Davoren, John, 189
Day, Doris, 32, 86, 220
De Marco, Nina, 23
De Marco, Renée, 20, 21, 24
De Marco, Sally, **20**, 21, 24, 59
De Marco, Tony, **20**, 21, 24, 59
Dean, James, 64
Della Chiesa, Vivienne, 242

Dellair, Don, 40-43, 45, 47-48
Desmond, Johnny, 200
Devore, Sy, 167
Dick Gasparre and His Orchestra, 59
Dick LaSalle and Orchestra, 100
DiGatano, Jayne and Adam, 59
Distel, Sacha, 200
Downey, Morton, 59
Draper, Paul, 27
Dreyfuss, Henry, 67
Duchin, Eddy, **25**, 26
Duchin, Peter, 26, **204**, 242
Dudevani, Avi 182-183
Durante, Jimmy, 152
Dusick, Kenneth Bruce, 152
Dusick, Ryan, 152

E
Ebb, Fred, 159
Eckstine, Billy, 242
Ed Sullivan Show, The, 64, 124, 132, 140, 171, 224, 228
Edwards, Blake, 146
Eisenhower, Dwight, 42
Ellington, Duke, 85, 106, 108-110, **111**, 112-114, 118, 121
Ellison, Ralph, 112, 113
Eloise, 11, 12, 14, 53, 77-83, 96
Emil Coleman Orchestra, 21, 27

Emmy Awards, 86, 91, 151, 208
Ennis, Ethel, 242
Evans, Bill, 85

F
Fabian, 66
Faith, Percy, 170
Farentino, James, 155-156
Fawcett, Farrah, 206
Fields, Dorothy, 151
Finklea, Tula Ellice. See Charisse, Cyd.
Fisher, Eddie, **180**, 181
Fitzgerald, Ella, 99, 183
Five Satins, 172
Flatt, Ernie, 159
Fontaine, Joan, 210
Ford, John, 146
Ford, Phil, 200
Four Saints, 84
Four Seasons, 172
Franchi, Sergio, 200
François, Jacqueline, 200
Freed, Clarence, 87
Froman, Jane, 100

G
Gardner, Ava, 14
Garland, Judy, 77, 95, 166
Garner, Errol, 242
Garner, James, 86
Garrett, Kelly, 242
Gary, John, 200
Gavin, John, 147
Gaye, Marvin, 205
Gaynor, Gloria, 205

Genevieve, 100
Gershwin, George, 147
Gibson, William, 151
Gilbert, John, 34
Gillespie, John Birks "Dizzy", 32
Gonsalves, Paul, 106
Gore, Lesley, 214-217
Goulet, Robert, 172, **195**, 200
Grammy Awards, 99, 141, 234
Grant, Cary, 32, 47, 197, 198
Gray, Arthur, Jr., 171
Greco, Buddy, **154**, 155
Greco, Dani, 155
Greenwood, Lil, 110, 115
Gregory, John, 149
Grimes, Tammy, 200
Gustavus V, King of Sweden, 40, 42

H
Haakon, Paul, 59
Haley, Bill, 66
Hamilton, Sam, 200
Harmon, Johnny, 194
Harris, Donna, 242
Harrison, Noel, 200
Hartman, Grace, **24**
Hartman, Paul, **24**
Hartmans, The, 27
Heatherton, Joey, 160
Henderson, Florence, 200, 242
Henry King Orchestra, The, 27
Hepburn, Audrey, 98

Hepburn, Katherine, 14
Herman, Jerry, 85
Hervey, Irene, 234, **235**
Hildegarde, 15, **30**, 39-40, **41**, 42-43, **44**, 45, 48, 80, **163**
Hilton, Ann, 242
Hilton, Conrad, 12, 67
Hines, Mimi, 200
Hodges, Johnny, 106, 113, 114
Holden, William, 146
Holdrege, Lee, 224
Holiday, Billie, 85, **104**, 109, 112, 114-116
Holm, Celeste, 49-50, **51**, 52-58, 127, 160
Hope, Bob, 100, 178
Horne, Lena, 183, 187, 198, 227
Houston, Josephine, 59
Howard, Leslie, 52
Hungry i, San Francisco, CA, 224

I
Ives, Burl, 100

J
Jack Paar Show, The, 171
Janssen, David, 155
Janssen, Ellie, 155
Jazz at the Plaza, 104-117
Jeffries, Fran, 201
John, Mr., 196-197, 225-227
Johnson Family Singers, 170

Johnson, Betty, **168**, 169-172
Johnson, Kenneth, **168**
Johnson, Lyndon, 198
Johnson, Marilyn, 242
Jones, Allan, 234
Jones, Jack, 133, 234, **235**, 236-238, **239**, 240-241
Jones, January, 242
Jones, Quincy, 215
Jones, Tom, 173

K
Kallen, Kitty, 200
Kander, John, 159
Kay, Monte, 95
Kay, Stanley, 153
Kazan, Elia, 51
Kazan, Lainie, 127, 181, 207-208, **209**, 210-211, **212**, 213-214
Kelly, Gene, 52
Kelly, Grace, 56
Kennedy, Jackie, 14, 95, 140, 237
Kennedy, John F., 14, 55, 95, 140
Kenzel, Cathryn, 172-173, **174**, 175-176
Kern, Jerome, 170
Kessler, Alice and Ellen, 200
Kind, Roslyn, 223-225, **226**, 227-228, **229**, 230
Kirby, Jack, 208
Kirk, Lisa, 68, 79-80, **83**, 84-85, **120**, 123-129, 135

Kitt, Eartha, 107, 121, 123-124, 127, **128**, 129, **163**, 213
Knight, Evelyn, 100
Knight, Hilary, 11, 14, 77, 79-84

L
Laine, Frankie, 146, 242
Lanchester, Elsa, 100
Lane, Abbe, 200, 242
Lane, Bobby, 194
LaRosa, Julius, 200
Larry Siry and His Orchestra, 59
Latin Quarter, 92
Laurette and Clyman, 59
Lawrence, Carol, 194, **195**, 196-198, **199**, 247
Layton, Joe, 179
Lee, London, 242
Lee, Michele, 151-153, **154**, 155-156
Lee, Peggy, 166
Leisen, Mitch, 150
Leo Reisman Orchestra, 26
LeRoy, Mervyn, 88
Leslie, Diane, 242
Lettermen, The, 161-162 165-167, 169, 176
Leverson, Peter, 236
Lewis, Jerry Lee, 66
Lewis, Jerry, 88, 176
Lewis, Luigi, 223
Lewis, Marcia, 157
Liberace, 37, 39, 40-45, **46**, 47-48, 64
Liebes, Dorothy, 67
Lilo, 100

Lipset, Ben, 144
Little Anthony, 216
Living Room, The, 236
Lopez, Trini, 216
Lor, Denise, 100, 200
Loring, Gloria, 200
Loudon, Dorothy, 200
Lydia and Jareaco, 27
Lynn, Leni, 59

M
Macero, Ted, 107
MacDonald, Kyle, 100
MacKenzie, Gisele, 243
Mackie, Bob, 210
Maharis, George, 100
Maltby, Richard, Jr., 224, **226**
Mancini, Henry, 76
Manulis, Martin, 91
Marcus, Stanley, 75
Marina (dog), **248**
Marina, Charlie, 243
Mario and Florio, 27
Mark Monte and His Continentals, 100
Markay, Grace, 200
Martin, Dean, 88, 167
Martin, Gail, 201
Martin, Hugh, 77
Martin, Tony, 201
Martino, Al, 243
Marx Brothers, 234
Mary Raye and Naldi, 100
Mason, Jana, 100
Mata and Hari, 100
Mattis, Laurie, 165
Matz, Peter, 92
Maurice and Cordoba, 59

– 254 –

Maurine and Norva, 27
McCabe, Sara Ann, 59
McCarty, Mary, 100
McDonald, Marie, 100
McGuire Sisters, The, 201
McNair, Barbara, 201
Mercer, Johnny, 76, 130
Merman, Ethel, 100, **163**, 201, 218, 236
Methuen, Paul, 76
Miller, Mitch, 183
Miller, Nolan, 98, 230
Miller, Susan, 59
Mills Brothers, The, 243
Mineo, Sal, 64, 100
Minnelli, Liza, 181, 182, **212**, 216, **239**
Mitchell, Bob, 164-165
Mitchum, Robert, 86
Mocambo nightclub, 68
Monro, Matt, 201
Moore, Phil, 92
Morgan, Helen, 88, 90
Morgan, Jane, 64, 100
Morison, Patricia, 68
Morse, Robert, 151
Morton, Gary, **163**
Morton, Vince, 164
Murray, Mae, 34

N

Newman, Phyllis, 92, 201
Newport Jazz Festival, 105
Norris, Bobbe, **145**, 201
Nype, Russell, 201

O

Orbach, Jerry, 155-156
Orbach, Marta, 155-156

P

Paar, Jack, 171
Page, Patti, 66, 189-192, **193**
Palmedo, Lillian Gaertner, **18**, 19
Pancho's Orchestra, 27
Payne, Cavril, 243
Peals, Jacques, 59
Peck, Gregory, 86
Perkins, Carl, 66
Peter Duchin Orchestra, 242
Pickens, Jane, 27
Pickford, Mary, 34
Plaza Hotel, New York, 11-12, **13**, 14, 19, **62**, 80, **138**, 149-150, 175, 186; advertisements, **13**, **22**, **30**, **41**, 104, 140, 143; Champagne Bar, 14, 80, 209; condominium conversion, 14, 38; doorknob, **190**; Oak Bar, 12, 179; Oak Room, 12, 40, 171-172; Palm Court, 12, 82, 169, 240; Rose Room, 14, 249
Porter, Cole, 68, 84, 124, 126, 127, 147
Powell, Jane, 201
Presley, Elvis, 64, 66, 205
Prowse, Juliet, 157-160

R

Rackin, Marty, 146
Radio City Music Hall, 247
Ramon and Rosita, 27
Rand, Jess, 165
Raniere, Katyna, 101, 201
Ray Benson Orchestra, 27
Ray, Johnnie, 64, 101
Reagan, Nancy, 217
Reagan, Ronald, 74, 217
Reams, Lee Roy, 157-160
Reiner, Carl, 151
Reisman, Leo, 26
Reyes and Los Chavales, 101
Reynolds, Debbie, 56
Rich, Buddy, 153
Rivero, Carmen, 59
Robinson, Jackie, 32
Rodgers, Richard, 92, 110, 147
Rolls, Rolly, 59
Rondina, Cathryn. See Kenzel, Cathryn.
Rooney, Mickey, 151
Roosevelt, Eleanor, 40, 41
Roosevelt, John, **25**
Rosario and Antonio, 59
Ross, Diana, 216
Rost, Henry, 19
Roth, Lillian, 101
Rothrock, Claire, 190
Rowles, John, 243
Rushing, Jimmy, 85, 106, 108-110, **111**, 112, 114, 115

Russell, Rosalind, 128
Russian Tea Room, 70
Ryan, D. D., 80

S
Sablon, Jean, 101
Sabrina (dog), **248**
Sanders, Felicia, 201
Sandler and Young, 91, 187, **188,** 189
Sandler, Tony, 187, **188,** 189
Sands Hotel, Las Vegas, NV, 153
Sanz, Ran, 243
Searle, Ronald, 81
Seay, Mr., **163**
Sell, Hildegarde Loretta. See Hildegarde.
Selznick, David O., 91
Sennett, Mack, 34
Severinsen, Doc, 243
Shay, Dorothy, 101
Shire, David, 224, **226**
Shore, Dinah, 32, **163,** 201
Shriner, Herb, 101
Silvers, Phil, 188
Sinatra, Frank, 14, 32 56, 77, 86, 115, 160, 167, 175, 201, 231
Skouras, Spyros, 148
Sonnabend, A.M., 67
Sonnabend, Paul, 213
Sosenko, Anna, 41
Spector, Phil, 215
Springer, John, 236
Springfield, Dusty, 243

St. John, Jill, 240
St. Regis Hotel, 144; Maisonette, 144, 206
Starr, Kay, 201
Sterney, George, 27
Stevens, Connie, 176, **177,** 178-179, **180,** 181
Stewart, Jimmy, 32
Strassard, Al and Dorothy, 147
Streisand, Barbra, 173, 208, 216, 223, 229
Stuarti, Enzo, 201, 243
Styne, Jule, 94, 129
Sullivan, Ed, 133, 142. See also Ed Sullivan Show.
Summer, Donna, 205
Swann, Russell, 59
Symington, Eve, 27

T
Taylor, Elizabeth, 14, 210
Ted Straeter and His Orchestra, 59, 71, 147
Temple, Shirley, 34, 183
Terry, Clark, 113, 114
Thompson, Kay, 11, 14, 66, 74-77, **78,** 79-83, 107, 127
Thunderbird Hotel, Las Vegas, NV, 234
Tony awards, 62, 92, 186
Towers, Constance, 144, 146-147, **148,** 149-150
Townsend, Irving, 106-109, 113-117
Tracy, Spencer, 14
Travis, Michael, 179
Travolta, John, 205

Truman, Harry, 42
Tucker, Sophie, 211
Tunick, Jonathan, 224
Tyler, Jeanne, 35

U
Uggams, Leslie, 183-184, **185, 186,** 187
Urban, Joseph, 18-19
USO, 178

V
Valente, Caterina, 201
Vallee, Rudy, 151
Van Dyke, Dick, 151
Van Vooren, Monique, 201
Veloz and Yolanda, 24-25, 35
Veloz, Frank, 24
Vignon, Jean-Paul, 130-133

W
Wagner, Robert F., 216
Waldorf Astoria Empire Room, 86
Walker, Nancy, 38
Wallis, Hal, 87
Wallis, Shani, 201
Wayne, John, 146
Wein, George, 105
Wells, Bob, 84
West, Mae, 70
Wheeler, Harold, 224
Williams Brothers, 74-75, **76,** 78, 107
Williams, Andy, 74-75, **76**
Williams, Mrs. Clarke, **163**

Williams, Roger, 243
Wilson, John C., 52
Wilson, John, 218, 237
Wilson, Julie, 67-68, **69**, 70-71, **72**, 73, 84
Winchell, Walter, 40
Windsor, Duke and Duchess of, 55

Wladziu Liberace. See Liberace.
Wonder, Stevie, 205
Wonder, Tommy, 47-48
Woodyard, Sam, 114
Wyman, Karen, 243

Y
Young, Ralph, **188**
Yukimura, Izumi, 201
Yvette, 101

Z
Ziegfeld Follies, 19

ACKNOWLEDGMENTS

It's with much gratitude and admiration that I thank and applaud the brilliant cadre of luminaries who so graciously shared with me their memories, impressions, and memorabilia related to gracing the Persian Room stage. I am especially grateful to those who told the stories of others who are no longer here to share their own recollections. As enchanting as the Persian Room was—and it was—it was still just a room. Its especially bewitching sparkle and luster emanated from the extraordinary parade of musicians, magicians, dance teams, comedians, singers, and other entertainers who passed through it with such style during the five decades when it was a New York City fixture. I'd especially like to express my deep affection and gratitude to Hilary Knight for his extraordinary assistance in providing background, suggestions, research, and inspiration.

I would also like to thank the smart, creative, and dedicated professionals who helped bring this book to life in such style; specifically, Ashley Prine for her brilliant Art Direction, Frank Vlastnik for his razor-sharp research and wizardry in locating those ever hard-to-find photographs, and Laura Ross for editing, and helping me pull it all together. Heaps of gratitude go out to Sujean Rim, for her inspirational cover and other illustrations that capture the exact essence of the times.

As always, a huge hug of appreciation goes to my angel Will Friedwald. Who, as always, brilliantly guided me through many of the musical nuances that transpired behind the scenes of this historic supper-club.

Thank you, without you all, this would be a less lively book, indeed. I'd also like to extend a special thank-you to the artists who provided me with photographs and artifacts from their personal collections.